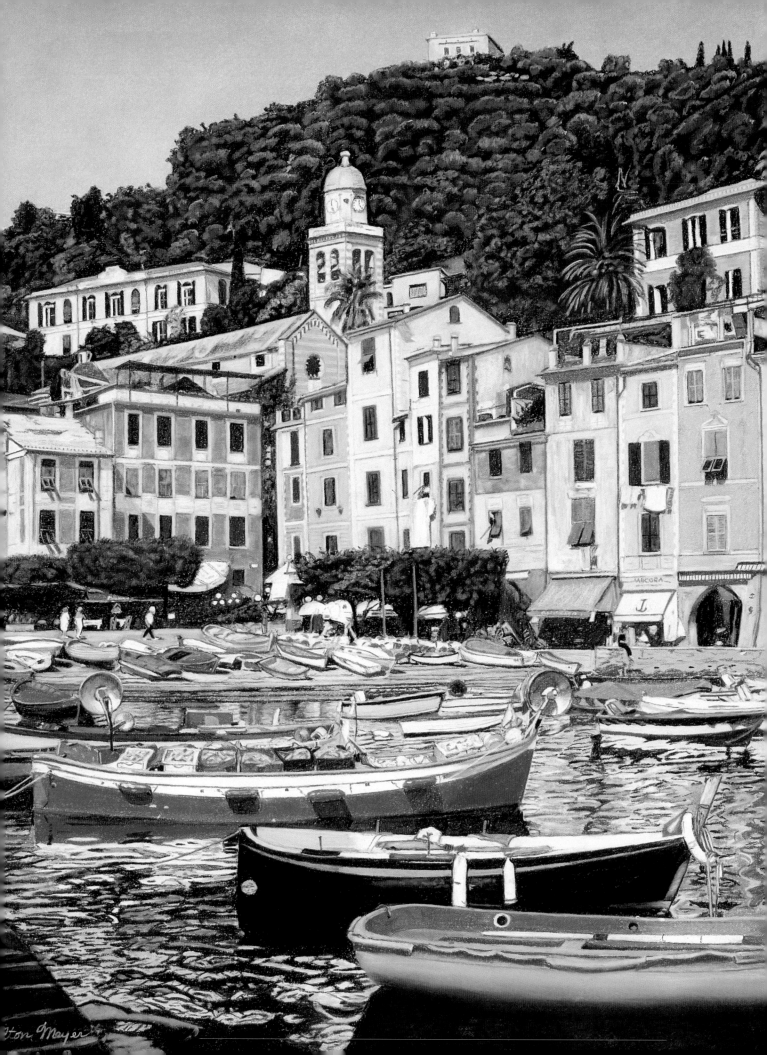

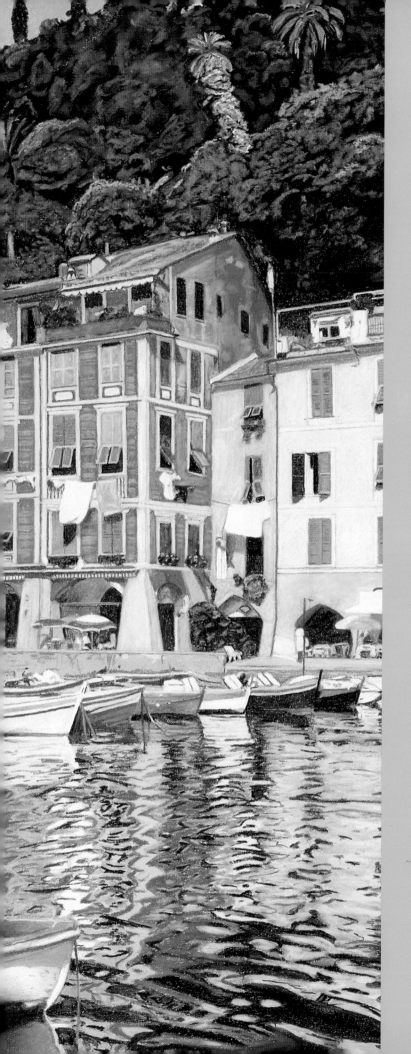

How to paint
WATER

Patricia Seligman

NORTH
LIGHT
BOOKS

Cincinnati, Ohio

A Quarto Book
First published in North America in
1996 by North Light Books,
an imprint of F&W Publications, Inc.,
1507 Dana Avenue, Cincinnati,
OH 45207
1-800/289-0963

ISBN 0-89134-706-2

Reprinted 1997, 1998

This book was designed and produced
by
Quarto Inc
The Old Brewery
6 Blundell Street
London N7 9BH

Senior Editor: Sian Parkhouse
Editor: Anna Selby
Senior Art Editor: Clare Baggaley
Designers: Vicki James,
Sallyann Bradman
Copy Editor: Helen Douglas-Cooper
Photographers: Paul Forrester,
Laura Wickenden,
Colin Bowling
Picture Researcher: Jo Carlill
Picture Manager: Giulia Hetherington
Art Director: Moira Clinch
Editorial Director: Mark Dartford

Typeset by Central Southern
Typesetters, Eastbourne
Manufactured in Hong Kong by
Regent Publishing Services Limited
Printed China by
Leefung-Asco Printers Ltd

Contents

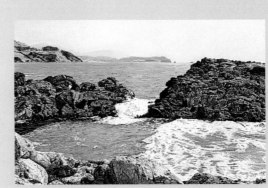

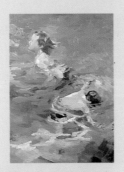

The Swimmers
(oil)
DENISE BURNS
Page 1

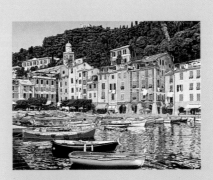

Portofino (pastel)
MILTON MEYER
Page 2

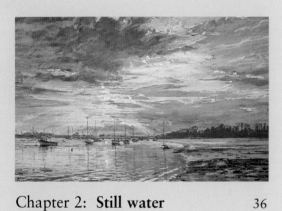

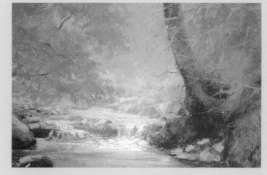

INTRODUCTION

Water is an alluring subject for those artists who look beyond themselves for subject matter. Its special characteristics of reflectivity and transparency and its ever-varied surface qualities pose a powerful challenge to artists of all abilities. Yet the appeal of water goes beyond the purely visual. It plays tricks with the light. And with its changing moods and its ability to mirror, distort, and fracture the world around it, it provides the perfect metaphor for human emotions. Some artists are sometimes put off by its reputation as a "difficult subject." Yet, like any other subject, it can be approached either in a systematic

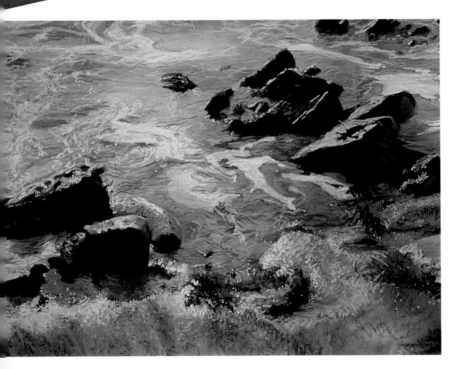

◀ **Rocky Shore No. 2** (pastel on sandpaper)
KITTY WALLIS
The evening light catching the swell and the swirl of the sea as it washes in between the rocks is captured with dancing pastel lines.

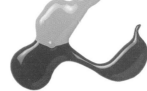

way that reduces the chances of failure; or in an intuitive way that exploits the sensitivity of water to weather and light and its potential for expressing human moods.

Water, wherever it is found, is unpredictable. A calm sea in a quiet cove can be whipped up into a monstrous swell with a change of wind direction or strength, or a deterioration in the weather. One day it gently laps the shore; on the next, it thunders with awesome power onto the rocks. Seen as a tidal wave or as part of a swollen, flooded river, such water represents nature at its most uncontrollable. It is this dark side of nature that draws many artists to water.

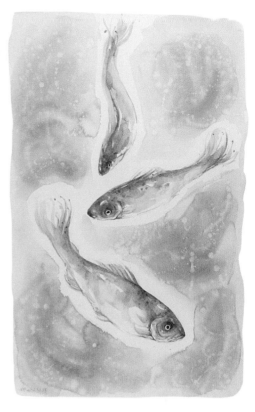

▲ **Three Fish Falling**
(watercolor)
RACHEL GIBSON
The fish are isolated in an aura of white against superimposed washes of blue, applied wet-on-dry and wet-in-wet.

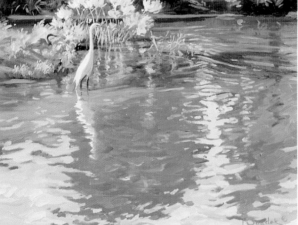

▲ **Sanctuary** (oil)
MARTHA SAUDEK
Interwoven horizontal strokes are built up to form the patchwork of reflections on this stretch of water.

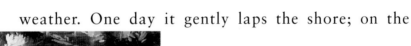

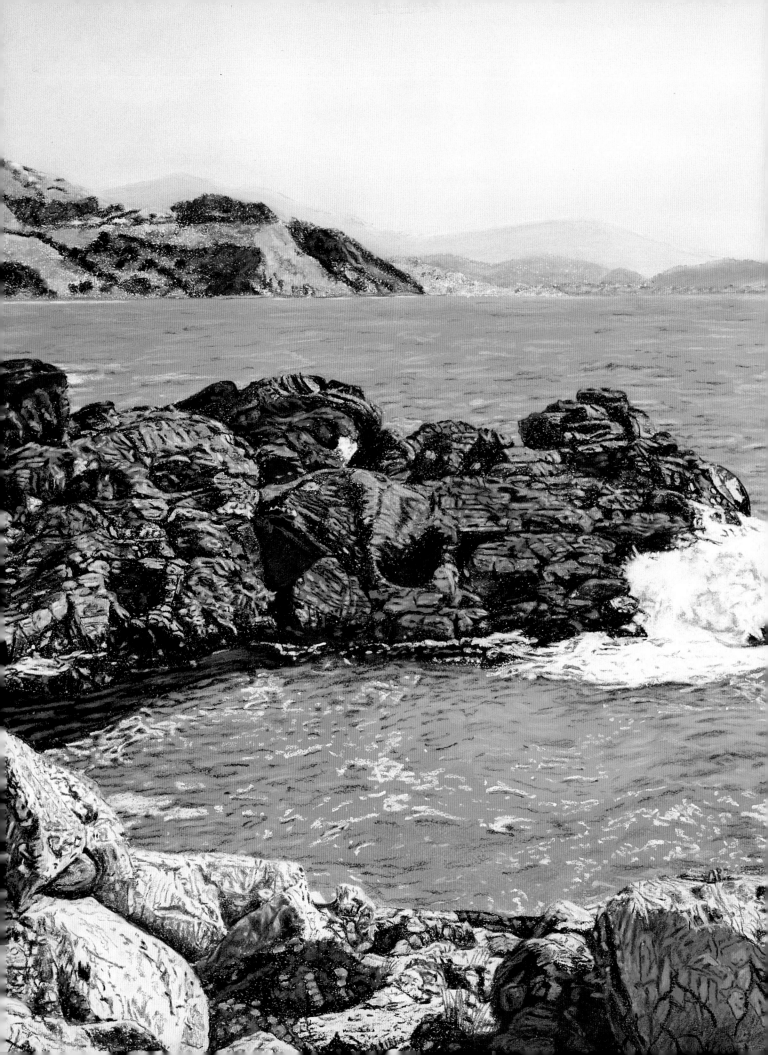

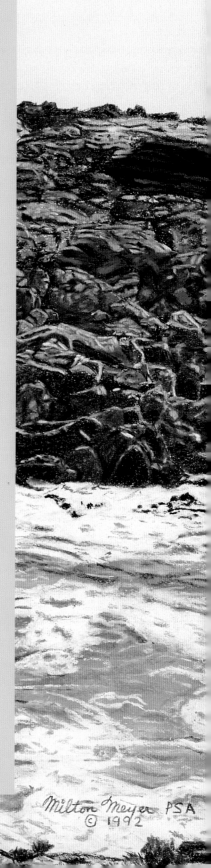

CHAPTER ONE

Getting Started

When painting water, the question often arises, "where do you start?" In fact, you can start almost anywhere: different artists have different theories. One will recommend a carefully worked out foundation drawing. Another will suggest an expressive under-painting. But what makes most artists hesitate from "getting started" is the profusion of detail in any waterscape. Here, we help you to work out how you can edit the scene to suit your purposes.

Restless Sea (pastel)
MILTON MEYER
In this picture, the artist has simplified the detail, giving the clues needed to read the pastel marks as a "restless sea."

Milton Meyer PSA
© 1992

Observing the subject

Wherever we live, we all have the opportunity to observe the behavior of water, even if only in the reflections and light refraction caused by a small boy splashing in a puddle, or street lights reflected in a glistening, wet sidewalk, or activity in the local swimming pool. Beyond scenes such as these close to home, there are ponds, lakes and rivers of all sizes, shapes, and colors – all affected by the weather and the seasons, while the sea, with its tides and moods, can be strikingly different in Reykjavik, Bali or Maine.

Many artists choose to live and work by water in order to study it in detail; others have to seek it out, coming across it while taking part in water sports or on vacation. A sailor once recounted how he would watch for hours on end the churning white water coming from the screws of the destroyer on which he worked, and how this inspired him to paint water subjects. Fishermen, through careful observation, understand the subtleties of currents and eddies in a river and the effect of light on the water, and some take up the brush.

Learning to look

To observe water is not, of course, the same as painting it, although the more looking and thinking an artist can do around a subject, the better. One of the greatest problems for an artist is to look at the world objectively: it is all too easy to paint what you think is there, rather than seeing what *is* there. Children think of the sea as blue, and although this is often the case, it is blue qualified by weed and stones on the seabed, sand and other particles suspended in the water, and white foaming water on the surface, reflections of the sky, and the sur-roundings. To see things as they are, rather than as we think and expect them to be,

takes great concentration. If you can teach yourself to look at water objectively, however, you will have gone a long way toward painting it well.

Looking at a scene with an artist's eye starts off as an intellectual exercise, with many questions being asked and, hopefully, answered. This cerebral dialogue, which may at first be rather forced, in time becomes second nature – a subconscious exercise. However, you have to work at it, training yourself to look. Observing a stretch of water, you might ask yourself: "Where is the light coming from?," "What quality is the light?," "What is the state of the water?," and "How reflective is the surface?" Your eye will dart around the scene, taking in information about composition and color, and you will be making decisions about possible mediums and techniques.

Sketching

To help train yourself to look carefully at a scene, it is worth spending time sketching waterscapes. You may find that pastels or watercolors are more useful than pencil or charcoal for capturing the fleeting light and immediacy of a waterscape.

A good exercise for teaching yourself to look objectively is to make individual

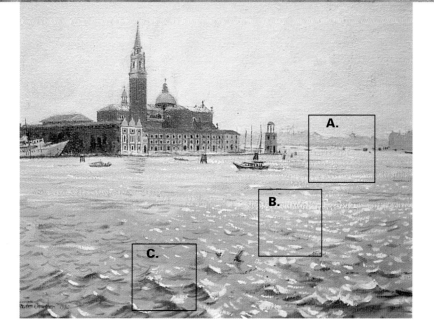

sketches of isolated patches of a waterscape, first in the foreground, then in the middle ground and then in the distance. You can focus in on these patches in the scene by using your hands as a viewfinder. If you are working from a photograph, cut a square hole in a piece of paper and mask off the rest of the scene. Force yourself to sketch each patch of water in isolation, seeing them as patterns of interlocking colors and tones. Comparing the three sketches, you will see subtle differences that your eyes might have skipped over or misread when observed as part of the whole scene. Now sketch the whole scene, making use of any new observations.

▲ **San Giorgio di Maggiore, Venice** (oil)

STEPHEN CROWTHER

Careful observation helps the artist to choose the most suitable medium and techniques with which to express himself.

Careful Observation

Painting in oils, the artist has chosen a view of San Giorgio di Maggiore seen across water that is shimmering in the evening light. The artist likes to work on the spot, often producing a pastel sketch that he works up in oils later. In this case the sky, water and reflected light had to be completed quickly, before the light died, to get the true relationships between them, but the buildings and ships were captured on camera.

The artist was attracted by the golden reflected light so the painting focuses on this aspect. Working down from the top of the painting, there is no detail in the distant water and the light is reduced to a layer of white drybrush over the base color. In the middle ground, the tonal range is narrower and the reflected light is limited to touches of highlight.

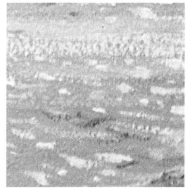

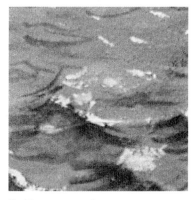

A. Distance

Here all detail in the water is lost, any turbulence is flattened out, and color and tone are reduced. The light on the water is captured in a broken layer of paint applied with a dry brush over the green-blue of the water.

B. Middle ground

Moving from distance to middle ground, the reflected light is expressed with a more broken drybrush stroke. It dissolves into white and yellow highlights and then into short strokes with a broader range of tone. Details are still not visible.

C. Foreground

The artist can now see the shape and movement of the choppy waves. These are described with lively strokes of the shadow tone and dry, chalky strokes of white superimposed over them.

Distilling the information

One of the more difficult aspects of painting any subject, particularly water, is the ability to capture the essence of the subject: that is, being able to glance at a view and see what needs to be included and what can be pruned away. You will see, in some examples, the graceful simplicity of certain images and the seemingly effortless way in which they have been formed with just a few strokes or by a simple combination of techniques.

Trying to capture the physical reality of the sea, a river or a pool, as well as a personal reaction to it, may sound like hard work. However, for most artists it does not require a conscious effort: the finished painting is itself a reaction to a particular view. However, working out precisely what you are trying to put across helps to pare down extraneous detail. To capture a scene's sparkling quality, you must edit down to its essential elements.

Editing the scene

This ability to edit a scene is a very real part of being an artist. Editing is not only a case of reducing a mass of detail, it can also entail "beautifying" the landscape – leaving out the pylons visible across the river, for instance. Or it may be a matter of changing the emphasis to make sense of the scene – including only the symmetrical screen of trees on a river bank and pruning out the less pleasing bushes that draw the eye away from the intended focus on the water.

Sometimes it is not enough just to paint what is there before you. Often the artist will subtly rearrange a scene or add to suit the composition. A mythical breeze might be introduced on a flat lake to break up the reflection. Similarly, it is quite common to combine elements from different occasions – boats from one visit, seagulls from another –

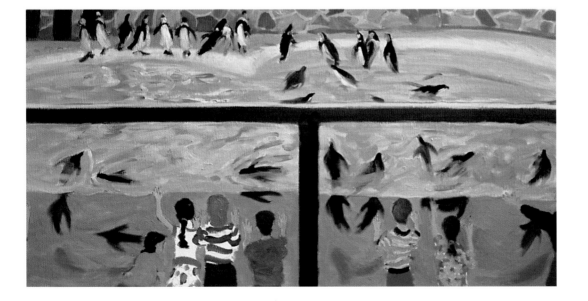

◀ **Twyford Zoo, Penguin Pool** (oil)
ANDREW MACARA
By reducing shapes and colors down to basics, we see the enjoyment of the children watching the penguins' antics. The water receives the most attention, with lively strokes on the surface and more blended strokes below.

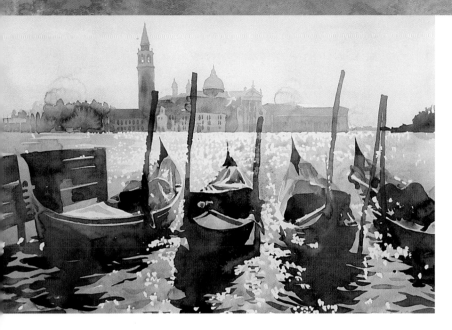

▲ **San Giorgio from Schiavoni** (watercolor)
HAZEL SOAN
The artist simplifies the color, the tones in the water, and the details in the screen of gondolas and background view in order to tell her tale.

but the information needs to be handled subtly so that a viewer of the finished painting does not question the veracity of the artist's vision.

Getting bogged down in detail

Even when you have edited a scene, it is still possible to get bogged down in detail. This usually happens because you are concentrating too hard on one area of the painting, putting in every ripple and wavelet, so that it looks out of focus compared with the rest of the work. If you have a tendency to make your work too detailed, try using a larger brush, or a broken pastel stick used on its side, together with a small support, so forcing yourself to simplify the image. Also bring on the whole painting at the same pace, guarding against working up any one area.

Editing the Scene
Concentrating on the reflections in the canal, and skipping over the detail of the surrounding architecture, work up the oily surface-swell of the water with pastels.

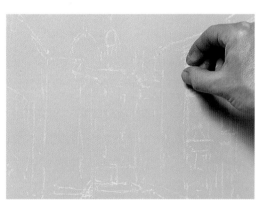

1 *Make a careful sketch in pale yellow, which will disappear under the pastel strokes.*

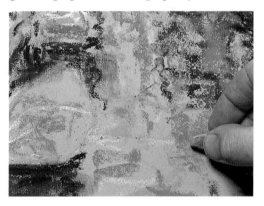

2 *To set the scene, block in color and tone over the whole surface of the picture.*

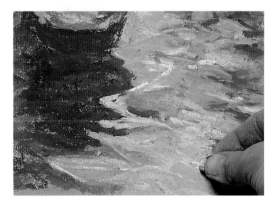

3 *Build up the color and tone, blending and then superimposing descriptive linear strokes.*

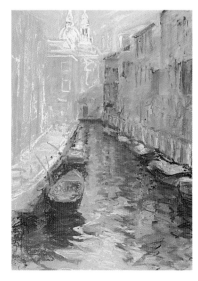

4 *Describe the buildings using fluent linear detail, and let the canal take the eye into the picture. If the water is worked on with a variety of techniques, building up color, tone and texture, it will grab the viewer's attention.*

Using photographs

There are occasions when photographs are a good way of studying water – particularly foaming, surging, splashing water that moves vigorously. However, while photographs can be a great help in learning about a subject, it would be unwise to use them exclusively as they usually show what happens in a split second of exposure and by freezing motion you can lose the essence of the surging mass of water.

Many artists now use a camera as they would a sketchbook – as a means of recording details. The disadvantage in this is that if you sketch a subject, you learn much more about its shape and texture, about the light shining on it, and more than you do by photographing it. However, sketching is not everybody's idea of fun. A camera can do the same job, and photographs can be used in the same way as sketches.

If you use a camera to record views of water, it is worth experimenting with the exposure time so that you capture not only the physical composition of the water but also its movement. Try setting the camera on a tripod and exposing the film for a few seconds. If you film white water in this way, you will find that it loses any hard edges, and this may give you some ideas for painting moving water.

Painting from photographs

Before you start painting from a photograph, take some time to analyze the composition as you would if you were sitting in front of the scene itself. The photograph can just be a starting point – a memory hook – reminding you of a scene, or you can compose the photograph carefully with a painting in view. Photographs are often too clear, with the background as focused as the foreground, as can be the case on a clear day. The artist, therefore, has to introduce the effects of aerial perspective in order to create a sense of

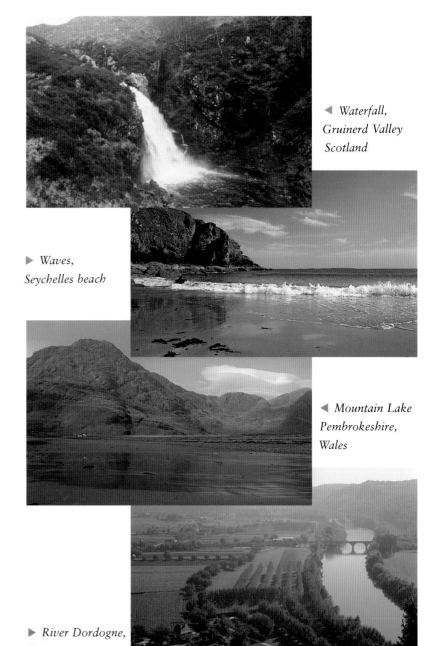

◄ *Waterfall, Gruinerd Valley Scotland*

▶ *Waves, Seychelles beach*

◄ *Mountain Lake Pembrokeshire, Wales*

▶ *River Dordogne, France*

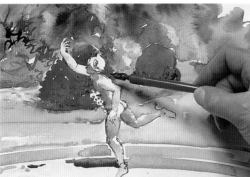

1 *First work on the background. Build up the foliage from paler washes wet-in-wet, to the darker bushes. Add the paths in a broken ocher wash.*

Editing a View

The artist has altered the proportions, extending the foliage upward and adding another topiaried bush. The bush behind Eros is expanded to set the statue against the dark foliage.

2 *Mix Hooker's green and ultramarine blue for the shadow, cutting in around the lilies with a square brush. Add touches of orange for goldfish.*

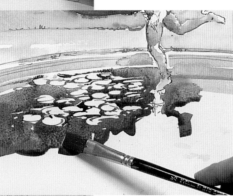

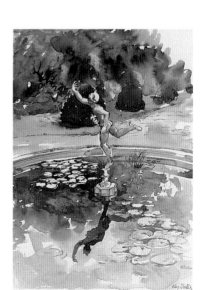

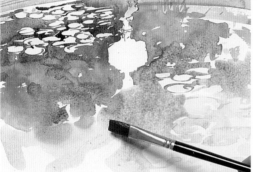

3 *While the shadow color is wet, wash in the sky so they merge. Leave random patches of white for cloud reflections.*

4 *Once the paint is dry, add a more concentrated shadow mixture at random around the water lilies.*

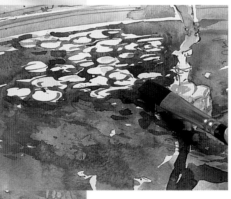

5 *With the same shadow mix, paint in the reflection of Eros, wet-on-dry with a fractured edge and broken color.*

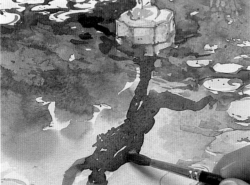

6 *The photograph has been edited and aspects exaggerated to make the painting work. Note how the colors are taken through – the foliage greens, touches of orange and yellow, to link the water with the background.*

Using photographs

All three of these photographs would make good paintings. And if you were not lucky enough to have taken them, you could use your knowledge of how water and light behave to interpret these scenes in your own way.

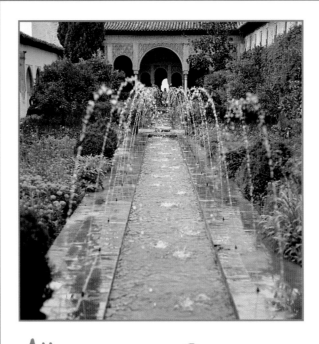

Alhambra Granada

1 *The photographer focuses on the Moorish loggia but, if you choose to focus on the water and spouts, details and color in the foreground will be stronger and the loggia a mere suggestion in the background. You may need to alter the viewpoint.*

recession into the distance.

Photographs often provide information that can be reorganized in order to strengthen a composition or to make a story clearer. For example, there might be more dramatic ways to describe a rushing river than how it appears in a photograph. You could use the information from a number of photographs, taking the best element from each. Take care, however, not to combine details taken from different viewpoints, or you may find yourself with confused perspectives. Scale, too, needs to be checked, and it is useful to try out various alternatives in thumbnail sketches before you start painting to see how your ideas work.

Reinjecting life

A perfect photograph can catch the moment and the mood – the waves glisten in the sunlight and the surf crashes down just as you remember it. These photographs are rare, however, and most of the time we are

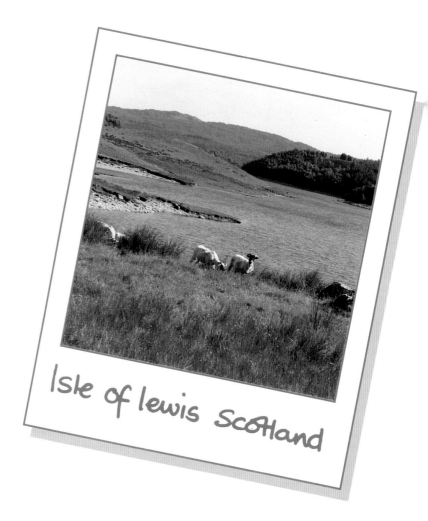

Isle of lewis Scotland

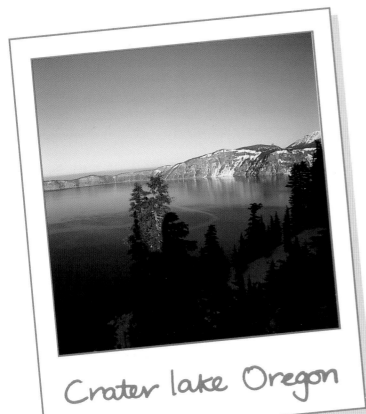

Crater lake Oregon

▲ **3** *A breathtaking site which could overawe the artist. The sun lights up the far side of the lake, visible through the foreground frieze of shaded trees, which could be tidied up. Be aware of a balance of verticals and horizontals and creating a sense of depth. Again clues are there to guide you. Note the different textures of the water and the curving "channel" taking the eye to the background. These elements are all worth working on.*

2 *Another photograph with potential but the water needs some life injecting into it. Exaggerate clues present – like the patches of darker water – and make the water more detailed closer to you or it will tilt up. Take touches of the landscape colors into the water to unite the two.*

working from sub-standard snaps taken with a foolproof camera, in inadequate light, using a film that is not quite appropriate and which is processed at a standardized setting. However, most of the time this is not important – your art is painting not photography – as long as you use your experience, and your memory of the moment recorded, to reinject life into the scene.

Water is particularly difficult to photograph because, unless the light is very good, the camera does not pick up the nuances of color and the sparkle on the surface. Touches of blue reflected in white water, ocher-yellow surges of peaty water, or purplish shadows, are all there if you look, but they are lost by the camera, which reduces them to a range of banal grays.

The camera, too, simplifies gradations in the tonal range, particularly in bright light. This can make it easier for the beginner to simplify the image, but it also destroys subtle passages of tone, and you will have to reinstate them based on your own experience. For example, an area of sea that appears dead gray in a photograph, filled with monotonous waves as far as the eye can see, can be recreated as it was – lively, pellucid, lapping against the boat – with dabs of broken color and the odd touch of surf to keep the eye moving across the canvas.

Emotional responses

It is easy to see how an artist can identify with the expressive nature of water: it can be rough or calm, angry or kind; it laps and babbles, roars and thunders. Water, in fact, expresses in a very physical way how we feel. A stormy sea with crashing waves is filled with drama and even doom. A lazy day at the shore, on the other hand, with children swimming and boats dipping at anchor offshore will evoke pleasure, warmth, and lassitude.

▼ **Icebergs at Ilulissat, Greenland** (oil)
KEITH GRANT
Stunningly beautiful icebergs linger with intent. The artist expresses such emotions with cold blues emphasized by contrasting areas of pink.

To see the extent to which color can affect the mood of a painting, try a simple experiment. Paint a simple water scene using predominantly pale pinks and pale warm yellows and blues; then paint it again, using hard, cold reds, greens and blues; and finally using colored grays. The first combination will give a painting a rosy, relaxed mood. Conscious use of warm colors such as cadmium red, ultramarine blue and yellow ocher, therefore, can produce feelings of calm. The second set of colors (lemon yellow, alizarin crimson and cerulean blue) gives a cold, unsettling feeling to a painting.

Harsh, bright colors jangle the nerves, more so if complementary colors are juxtaposed (red and green, yellow and purple, orange and blue). Undistinguished grays depress the spirits – yet such a painting can nonetheless be haunting or touching because of the emotion it evokes.

The experiment shows how color can help the artist to manipulate mood. Good paintings are not necessarily of happy, sunny days, although these may be easier to live with, but memorable paintings usually exercise the emotions and feed the soul.

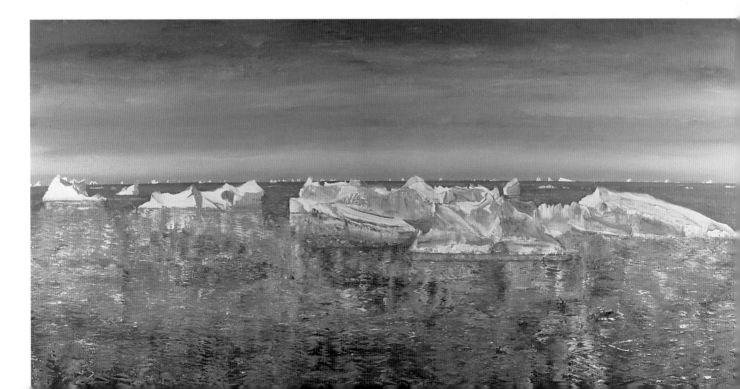

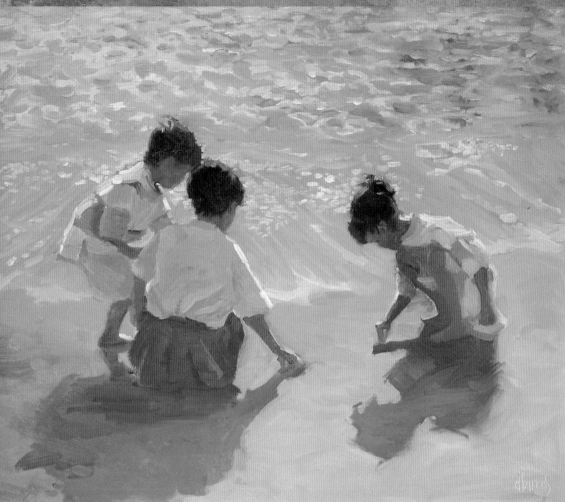

◄ **Sunwashed**
(oil)
DENISE BURNS
*Security and
innocent play are
underwritten in this
happy family scene
by the warm tints
of the evening sun,
and the gentle
lappings of the sea
on the shore.*

Weather

A painter of water to a certain degree becomes a painter of weather: sunlight and blue skies shining down on limpid seas, clouds racing along over turbulent water, invisible winds tossing the waves, and early morning mist hanging over silent, still water. Changes in weather in turn affect the quality of light, which is a very important controller of mood. Water reflects the smallest amount of light and can turn the last moments of a cold winter sunset into a festival of light.

Technique and mood

Mood can also be enhanced by technique. Try translucent glazes, bold, juicy strokes or agitated directional lines. Experiment using a painting knife to produce the flat calm of a lake, and then repeat the scene agitating the surface with short, interwoven strokes.

The warm colors on the top line can raise the emotional temperature. The cool colors in the middle can be used to project a cold, unsettled feeling. Juxtapose complementary colors, bottom line, for areas of tension.

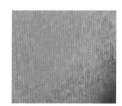

alizarin crimson

cobalt blue

lemon yellow

cadmium red

French ultramarine

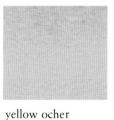

yellow ocher

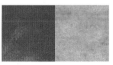

cadmium   viridian
red

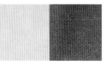

cadmium   mauve
yellow

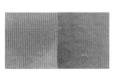

orange   cobalt
blue

If you live near water that is responsive to the elements – a river, lake, or the sea – try keeping a sketchbook diary of the weather and seasons. You will be able to see from it how your emotional response to a piece of water can vary.

Try sketching with different media – watercolor, acrylics, oils, pastels, colored crayons – to record your reactions. Take special note of the color of the light, emphasizing this in your sketches. Keen sketchers are not deterred by the vagaries of the weather and have been known to work with sketchbook and pencil in a rain-spattered plastic bag, or to use the rain to work with water-soluble pencils.

Controlling the mood

It is often possible to sense a certain mood in a scene, but it will need a little dramatizing in order to put it across. Sometimes this can be done by manipulating the tonal key of the painting. If you are painting a scene in a nondescript light that produces colors of a mid-tonal value, you can lift it by painting in colors at the lighter end of the scale. Painting in low-key tones will have the opposite effect. The relationship between the values in the scene you are painting need not alter, just the pitch of the values. If, for example, you are painting waves crashing onto a beach, pitch the value down and the scene will become brooding and ominous; pitch it up, and it will become more optimistic and frivolous.

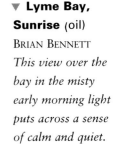

▼ **Lyme Bay, Sunrise** (oil)
BRIAN BENNETT
This view over the bay in the misty early morning light puts across a sense of calm and quiet.

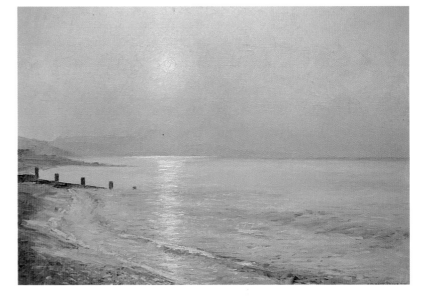

Expressive watercolor techniques
Watercolor, often thought of as tame, lends itself to expressive techniques. Here it captures the drama of the weather in the western isles of Scotland.

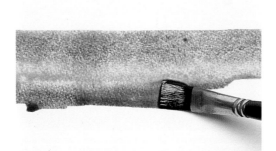

1 *The horizon is drawn in with a pencil and ruler, less than halfway up the support. Now wash over the sea area with a strong wash of Payne's gray and ultramarine blue and a large soft brush. Leave random areas of white paper for highlights and flick on extra color to vary the wash. Note how this mix granulates as it dries giving the area extra texture.*

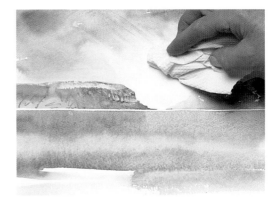

2 *Now add the isles in the background letting the brown spread into the sea to connect the two. Be brave with the sky using strong mixes of burnt umber, Payne's gray, and ultramarine, applied wet-in-wet and moving it around by manipulating the paper. Lift off the patch of light on the horizon with clean paper towels using diagonal strokes.*

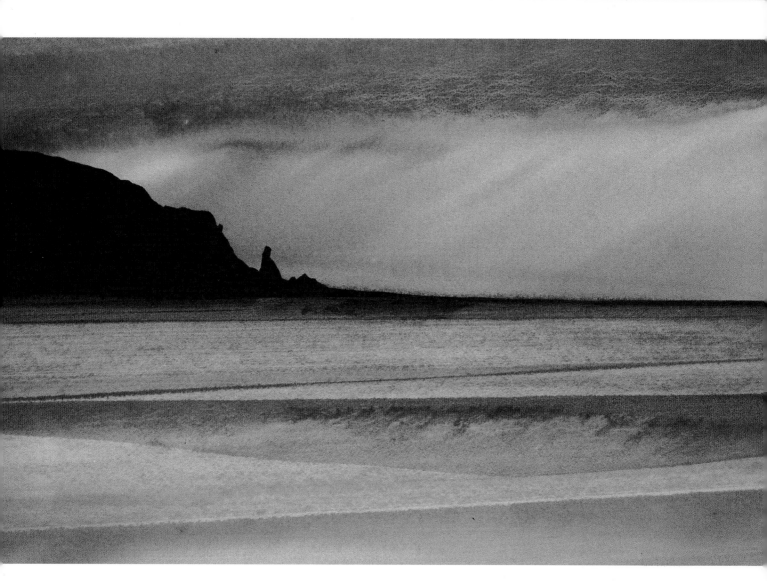

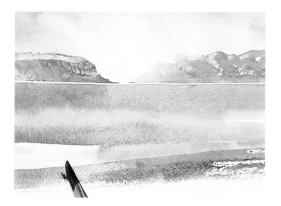

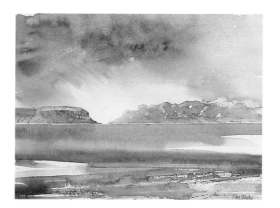

3 *With the water area dry, add the foreground in strong dry strokes of Payne's gray and burnt umber. Add enough paint to take the stroke across but sweep it across quickly so that it is broken up by the texture of the paper.*

4 *Learning to lay such dramatic washes takes practice, but even the most experienced artist has to know how to cope with the unexpected. You have to work fast one moment manipulating the paint before it dries and then the next, wait with patience for the paint to dry – all part of the diversity of the medium.*

▲ **Distant Tide, Winter**

(watercolor)

ROBERT TILLING

The brooding, rain-streaked sky as well as the dark and cold colors give this painting a disturbing air which is intriguing.

Composing a picture

So many paintings in this book look just right that you might think waterscapes compose themselves. However, it is not simply a matter of painting what you see. You need to give some thought to selecting a view, and creating a good composition to help the viewer to "read" your painting. Knowing how to manipulate the way a viewer looks at your painting puts you in control.

It is always well worth while spending time on composition. Whether you want to lead the viewer gently into a peaceful lakeside scene, using compositional lines to a single focal point like a castle on a hill or disturb him by introducing a number of focal points that vie with each other for attention, you will do it by the use of perspective, compositional lines, color, and tone.

Where to start

The first decision you have to make is about the shape and size of the support – the paper, canvas, or board on which you are going to work. This will depend on how you want to tackle the waterscape in mind. Portrait-shaped supports (taller than they are wide) are the natural choice for compositions with strong verticals such as tall-masted boats, waterfalls, and fountains; landscape-shaped supports (wider than they are tall) are better for horizontal views such as marinescapes that look out to sea, or river banks. An original view of water, however, can often be found just by avoiding the obvious. You can try out some thumbnail sketches to see how the composition might look in various shapes.

The size of your painting will depend on what you are trying to put across and who you are trying to impress. Small does not necessarily mean insignificant. "Six-footer" canvases by the English painter, John Constable (1776–1837), such as *The Haywain*, are impressive, but one of his tiny oils on canvas of the seashore at Osmington Bay, measuring only 9⅛ × 12⅛ inches, has a sense of freshness and immediacy that is hard to beat. Of course the size of the support will also depend on your location, your style of painting, and to a certain extent your experience. Large paintings are usually best tackled at home or in the studio, although not everyone is put off by the problems associated with carrying and setting up a large canvas in the open. To start with, however, choose a size that you think you can tackle comfortably in one session.

▼ **Low Tide, Lyme Regis II**
(watercolor and gouache)
JEAN CANTER
The natural lie of the seashore creates a grid of intersecting diagonals. These are emphasized by the light on the water, taking the eye deep into the picture space.

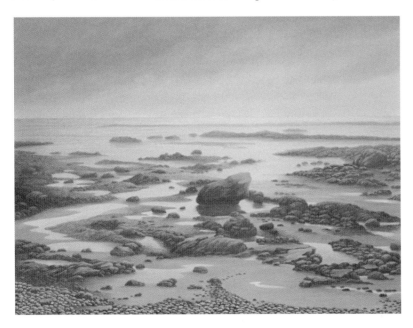

**Options in
Composition**

*A famous view of Venice
can tax the artist who wants
to be original. Thumbnail
sketches, trying out different
ideas in small, simple
drawings, can help. Here
the artist considers the shape
of the support, the cropping
of the subject, the
compositional lines, the
balance of the composition,
and the emphasis on the
water. He then tries out a
few ideas to see if they work.*

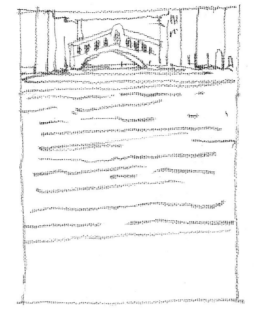

A portrait format emphasizes the water.

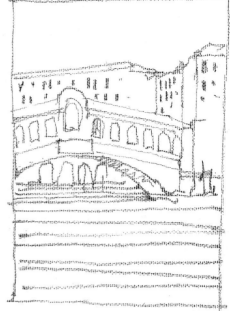

Cropping the bridge gives an unusual view.

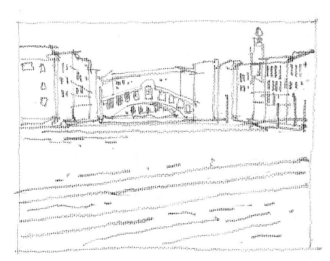

The background symmetry is offset by diagonal waves.

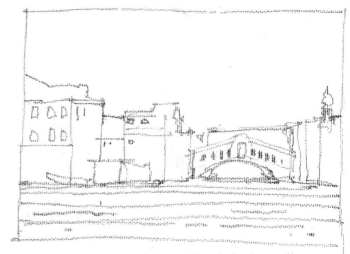

Sky, land and water are balanced, but the bridge is offset.

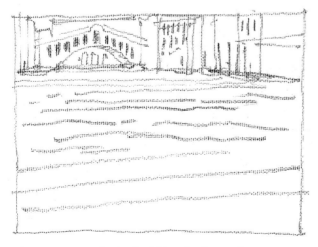

The water is emphasized within a landscape format.

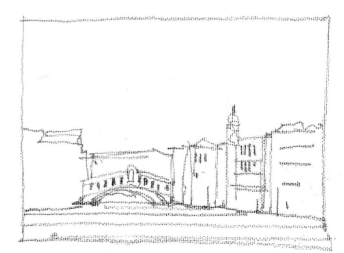

A shift of focus to the sky prompts the question: is it Venice?

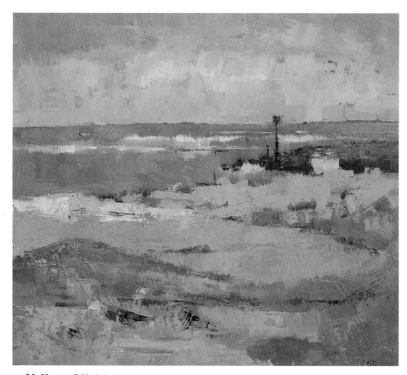

▲ **Yellow Oilskin** (oil)
JOAN ELLIOTT BATES
The eye is drawn by the yellow figure, and then subtly led around the canvas by delicate echoes of yellow-tinted grays.

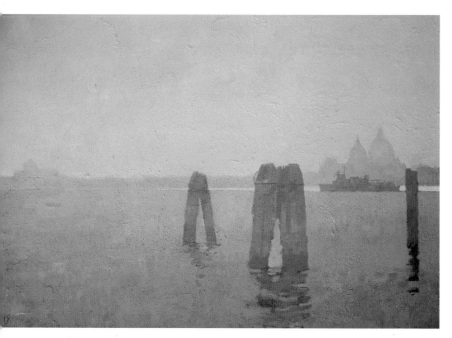

▲ **Channel Markers** (oil)
PETER KELLY
These channel markers act as vertical balances to the horizontals in the composition. They also divert attention, initially, from the famous Venetian landmark in the background.

Placing the horizon

Many painters of water claim that the placing of the horizon is the most important aspect to get right, and that once in place, everything else will slot in. The horizon level depends on your viewpoint. If you are looking down on a seascape from the top of a cliff, the horizon will be high in the picture, whereas, if it is seen from the viewpoint of a flat beach, the horizon will be low.

The placing of the horizon has a palpable effect on the mood of a painting. When you are next looking out over a stretch of water, try some sketches of the same scene with high and low viewpoints, and you will see why it is that so much importance is given to this one aspect of the painting. In the end, the horizon level will depend on what you are trying to put across in a work. If you want to focus on the water itself and its physical appearance, it would be sensible to place the horizon higher up the picture area, or to exclude it altogether. If you want to put across a feeling of the vastness of an ocean, then bring the horizon down.

Adjusting the view

You can alter the composition of a view radically by the way that you crop it. Try looking at the scene through a viewfinder formed with your hands or cut out from a piece of card. Move it around the scene, focusing on details such as an interesting boat or an area of pondweed, looking from left to right, and straight ahead. You will soon see what the options are and what, to you, seems the most appropriate view for your needs. The search for an original viewpoint will not only challenge your creativity, but will cause the viewer to re-assess what may be an ordinary scene. You could try viewing the scene at a sharp angle: at the seaside, this will mean that the waves will come into the shore on the diagonal instead of in parallel horizontal lines.

The cropping of a scene is also worth attention. A gaggle of fishing boats in a harbor can become an interesting study in

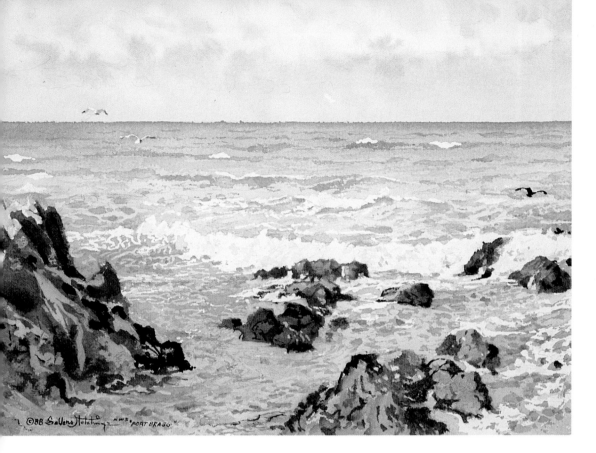

(watercolor)
LaVere Hutchings
The eye is initially attracted by the rocks and broken waves in the foreground and is then led into the distance through patches of tonal contrast provided by white-crested waves and seagulls. Note how the birds are made to stand out, painted light against dark in some places and dark against light in others.

positive and negative shapes through imaginative cropping. If you crop across the horizon on both sides of the scene, this will work against any feeling of depth (see below).

Focal point

One of the more common problems associated with compositions of water scenes concerns the choice of a focal point. A view out to sea, or across a lake, or a stretch of river, often has no obvious center of interest. The artist therefore has to make one, and this can be done in a number of ways. The eye is drawn by anything that stands out from the rest of the painting. This might be a vertical in a view of mainly horizontal compositional lines, like a boat at anchor at sea. It could be provided by a contrast of tones – a patch of light against a dark shadow or vice versa, maybe a wave caught as it breaks; or it could be provided by a small splash of a bright, advancing color like yellow or red – a figure on a beach, for example, or a red sail. Alternatively, impasto brushwork will catch the light and attract the attention

where it occurs on a smoother background.

Having decided on the focal point, you next need to lead the viewer's eye to that point. The artist usually does this through a combination of visual "tricks." Strong directional lines in the composition can point the way around the picture space, and these can be emphasized or complemented by directional brushwork, along which the eye tends to travel. Or the eye can be drawn by a pathway of color accents or tonal contrasts. Using all these devices, the artist can work toward animating the canvas, leading the eye on a merry dance across and into the picture space.

Aerial perspective

The sense of space and distance that a stretch of water can provide is what attracts many artists to the subject in the first place. Yet putting across the vastness of the ocean can be tricky. Water seen in the distance will show the effects of aerial perspective: outlines will become increasingly blurred, detail will be reduced, and colors will appear more

Aerial Perspective: Blending Oils

To create a sense of distance, decrease clarity, detail, tone, and color strength in the distance. The easy way of blending oils, used here to kill clarity, color and tone, immediately instills a sense of perspective.

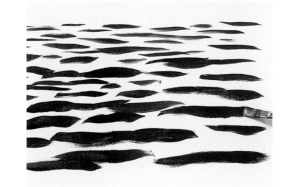

1 *Using black, and starting from the top of the water area, dab on small, horizontal strokes, making them smaller in the distance than in the foreground.*

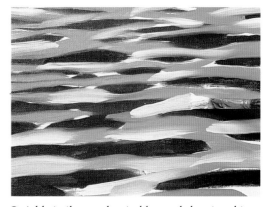

2 *Add similar strokes in blue and then in white, wet-in-wet, letting them merge with the strokes beneath and leaving patches of white canvas showing through.*

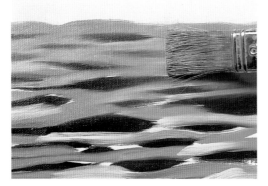

3 *Now take a large, soft brush that is both clean and dry, and gently stroke it over the top third of the water, blending the strokes of color – but not too much.*

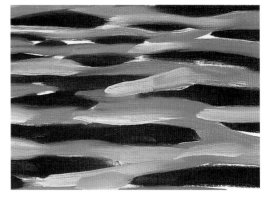

4 *This soft blending creates the effects of aerial perspective, blurring and flattening the details, reducing the tonal extremes and knocking back the color.*

and more bleached and blue the farther away they are. In a seascape this means that waves that are rough in the foreground appear to flatten out the farther away they are, and the color of the sea appears bluer and the tonal ranges narrower and paler. Failure to include the effects of aerial perspective, and at times to exaggerate them, can lead to a stretch of water appearing to tilt upward on the canvas.

Perspective of waves and ripples

Another cause of "tilting" water is the failure to observe that waves and ripples which are parallel to the picture surface appear closer together the farther away they are, until they merge into a seemingly flat area of water. This effect increases as the viewpoint gets lower. Ripples from a central splash move outward in concentric circles, but the same applies when they are seen from a lower viewpoint.

Waves seen from the side will behave like parallel lines at right angles to the picture plane, converging to a vanishing point on the horizon. However, remember that only the waves in the foreground will have any form or detail.

Scale

Another way of suggesting that water reaches to infinity is by including an indicator of scale: by including an element in the composition that is a recognizable size in relation to other elements – like a figure, a boat, a lighthouse or a rock. If this indicator is represented as minute within the framework of the composition, it will suggest a sense of vastness and distance. For example, if you include a very small figure quite close to the foreground on a beach, and there are headlands running into the sea in the middle ground from both sides, and then the sea beyond, the figure will suggest the vast scale of the scene and the eye will be led into the depths of the picture space through the landscape.

Starting to paint

There are many ways to approach the early stages of a painting. Some artists like to make a careful, finished sketch for the work, while others like to keep their options open and only roughly paint in the main compositional lines as a guide. Time taken over a sketch can save much aggravation later on as the sketch forces you to make decisions about the composition at the start.

After the sketch, the first layers of paint

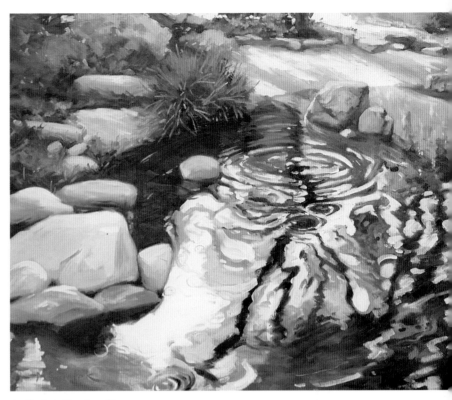

▲ **Quiet Pool** (oil)

MARTHA SAUDEK

Concentric circles of ripples spreading out from the rise of a fish or a thrown pebble are seen in perspective, as ellipses.

are important in releasing your inhibitions, blocking in the main areas of color and tone, and for setting the mood. You can help yourself envisage the painting by retracing the sketch with local color. This process is more common for opaque mediums such as acrylics and oils, but even with watercolors it is useful to cover the whole area with pale underwashes, mapping out the composition to break the ice.

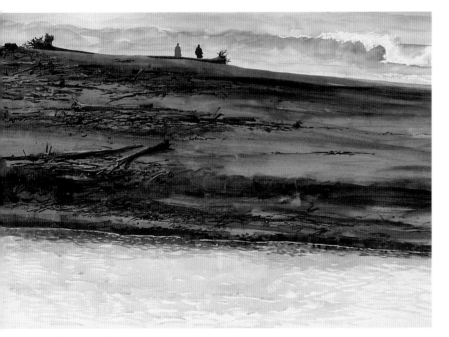

▲ **Gualala Sandbar** (watercolor)

BRYN CRAIG

The composition is initially hard to decipher but gradually unfolds. When the figures are located, they set the grandeur of the scale, leading the eye to the crashing wave.

Oil

Oil paints normally lend themselves to portraying water – the juiciness of the paint has a natural glint which reflects light rather in the way that water does. Combine this natural characteristic with the ability to build them up, one transparent layer over another, and you are halfway to painting water. Oils are particularly suitable for painting moving rivers and the sea, but you will find inspiring oil paintings of all types of water.

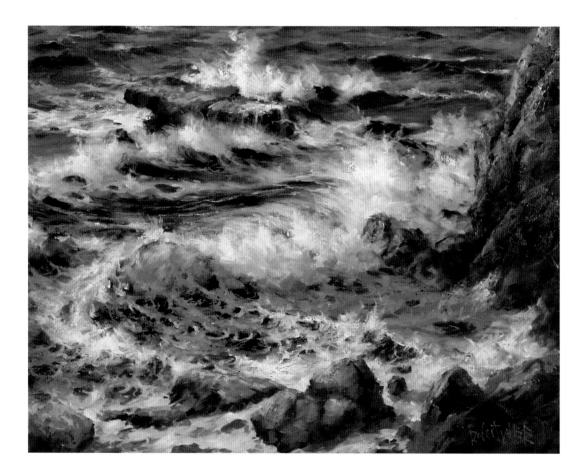

Wave Battered Rocks (oil)
ROBERT WEE
Using both the transparent and the opaque qualities of oils to build up the color of the water, superimpose with areas of white water at the crests of the waves and in the flying surf. The earlier applications are more diluted with turpentine, the later ones drier and thicker.

Oils can be used in many different ways – *alla prima* (see page 70), where the painting is finished in one sitting, applying the paint wet-in-wet. Alternatively, you can build up the painting carefully in layers, leaving one layer to dry before applying the next wet-in-dry. Glazing over the whole area of water after the painting is dry with transparent umber or ultramarine mixed with a glazing medium can help to give an area of water a cohesive, reflective surface.

Most artists find they can mix most colors from a basic palette. Look at those on the opposite page and those used by the artists in the demonstrations on pages 82–89, 116–119 and 136–141 for more ideas. These colors all have their own characteristics: transparent or semi-transparent; warm or cool; and some have a strong tinting power, meaning only a little is needed when mixing. Some dry more quickly than others, though you can add a medium to speed up drying.

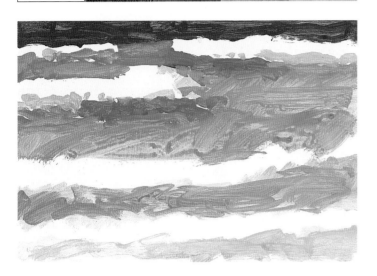

A scene of rollers breaking is simply conveyed in this oil sketch. The movement of the water is captured with directional brushstrokes with darker layers superimposed over more dilute ones creating variations in the tone. This is lighter in the foreground and darker in the background to create an illusion of recession. Mixes of monestial blue, cerulean blue, cadmium yellow, Payne's gray and white create the band of tones represented here.

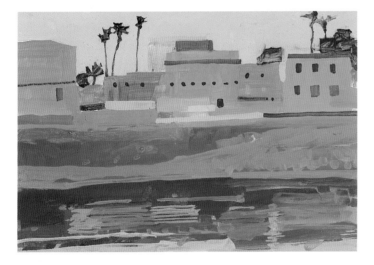

The heat of the sun and the dark murkiness of the water comes across in this sketch. Although the water has been painted wet-on-wet, the artist has been careful to place each brushstroke carefully so that this area of subtle neutral colors does not deteriorate into a confused mess. The area of water is given cohesion by keeping the strokes horizontal. The sky reflection – cerulean blue and white with a touch of black – is painted into the neutral grays below so that the color is less bright, as it would be in a reflection.

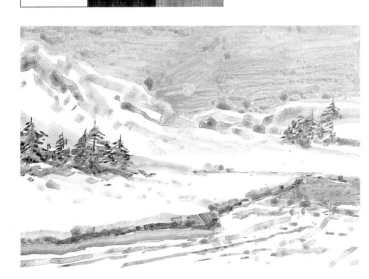

Deluxe mixes of cerulean blue, black and white map out this January scene with a frozen stream in the foreground. Start with the sky and the paler shadows in the snow. Then carefully add the mid-tone shadows, finally add the darker ones, the trees and the course of the river. Keep the brushstrokes crisp using the square shape of the flat brush. Finally superimpose slightly thicker pale strokes over the pool of water to represent the ice.

Acrylic

Acrylics are opaque water-based paints. They dry quickly, making them particularly useful for building up successive layers wet-on-dry, and so are a good choice for painting water. They can be diluted with water and used like watercolors with a glazing medium for a rich glint or used straight from the tube to build up thick impasto brushstrokes.

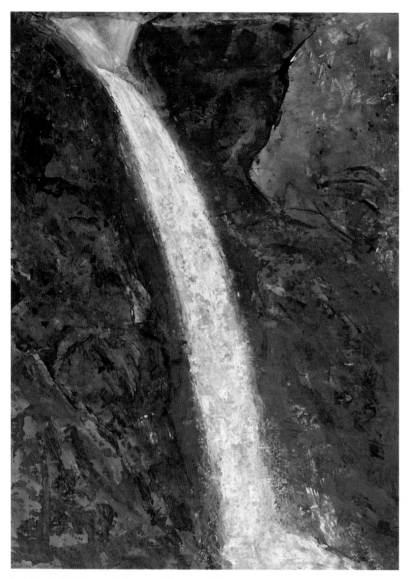

Waterfall, Gran Sabana, Venezuela
(acrylic and watercolor)
KEITH GRANT
As acrylics are waterbased, they can be used over other waterbased paints – here over a watercolor underpainting. The "white" waterfall is scumbled in acrylic over greens and purples to create the falling body of water.

For sketching in situ on the water, acrylics are particularly useful as they are so adaptable and can be used diluted or not, on paper, canvas (prepared or not), or wood. Fresh water from the river or stream can be used to dilute them so you don't even have to carry that. You can use them in your sketchbook but remember that the paper absorbs the first application of paint, almost priming it. So, if you want to build the paint up, let the first layer dry before using thicker paint. Try using them combined with pastels, too.

You can mix most colors and having a limited palette gives your painting a certain unity. Try to choose your colors with warm and cool in mind so that you can balance and contrast them. For instance, you would have a warm blue (such as French ultramarine) and a cool blue (such as monastral or phthalo-cyanine blue – equivalent to the traditional Prussian blue).

There is a great choice of available whites – titanium white, which is most commonly used, is good and opaque, making it perfect for building up areas of impasto white water. Zinc white, which has a blue tinge, is much less opaque and is therefore more useful for glazing a milky film on water as you might see on the edge of the seashore, or for knocking back water which is too bright and clear and comes farther forward in the picture than intended. Flake white is a silver white and is not as heavy as titanium.

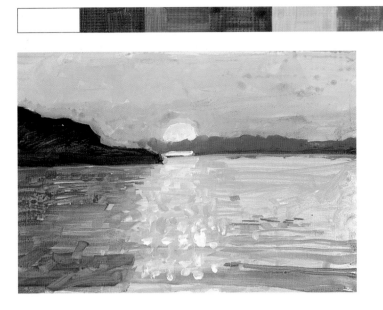

Acrylics are useful for capturing a fleeting light. In this sketch of the setting sun reflected in a golden path, first map out the water quickly in a dilute, uneven layer of pthalo blue, cadmium yellow and white. This layer is very thin and will dry quickly but the next layer can be superimposed wet-in-wet with darker strokes of the same mix with touches of maroon added. The golden reflected path is built up with clean impasto strokes of mixes of cadmium yellow and orange, maroon and white added wet-in-wet.

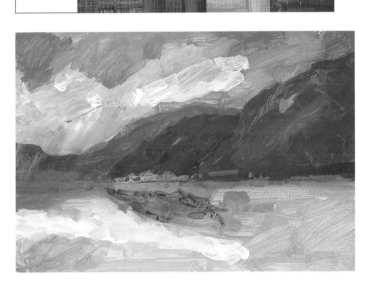

Another acrylic sketch explores a more expressive use of the medium. The cloud and mountain reflections are left as separate elements in the water, emphasizing the symmetry and bringing out the abstract potential of this moody scene. For the water, thin washes of white, monestia blue and ivory black are qualified by transparent glazes of yellow ocher mixed with monestial blue for the mountain reflection and opaque white and ivory black for the cloud.

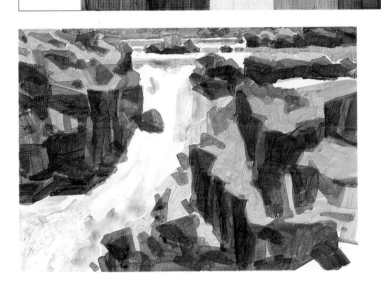

Keeping shapes simple in this scene of water crashing down between the rocks means identifying areas of light and shade which can be mapped out with a pencil first. Sap green, pthalo blue with a touch of Payne's gray make the water shadows, feeding the paint on so that it dries unevenly. Let the off-white paper represent the "white" water and when the shadows are dry, scumble over pure white with a coarse brush to put across the energy of the falling water.

Pastels

Pastels – either chalk or oil – are perfect for painting water, as you will see from the many examples in this book. With chalks, the underlying color of the water can be blended, with bright accents of more linear color to define highlights and reflections on the surface. Oil pastels can be blended with turpentine for water-like movement.

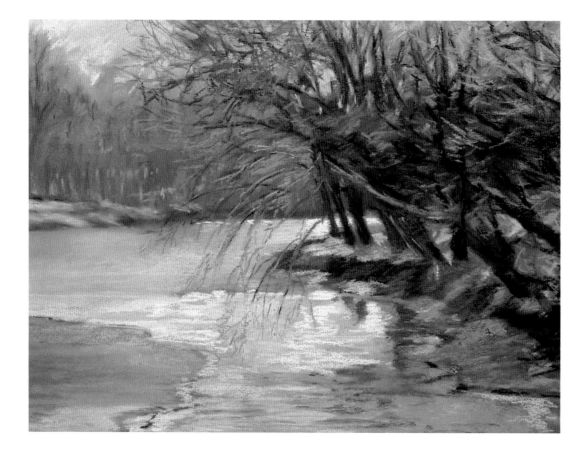

Cedar River
(pastel)
L.C. LAIRD
Reflecting the cold evening light, the sluggish river breaks through the rice. Pale yellow and pink reflected light is scumbled over the textured paper and contrasted with blended grays and browns in the shadows.

You can buy special pastel paper, which has a rough and a smooth side, and comes tinted in a variety of shades. The tooth breaks up the pastel stroke letting the tinted paper show through. This is particularly useful in judging tonal relations because you can use the paper as the mid-tone and add shadows and then highlights. With oil pastels you can paint a layer of turpentine onto prepared paper and then work the pastels into it, adding more turpentine with a brush when it gets too dry.

Pastels come in tints of the most popular colors of other media; you may find it easiest to buy a ready-made selection and then choose a few for the particular scene you have in mind. Hold a few in your free hand, changing them as you move on to a different part of the painting. Try and keep your colors fresh without too much mixing although you can combine colors optically by scumbling a thin film of a lighter color over a darker one (yellow over red to make orange), or by stippling, with adjacent dots of color.

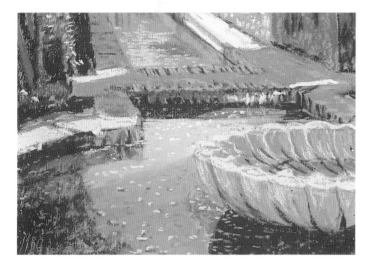

A combination of shadows and reflections on still ornamental ponds creates a challenge for the artist. The contrasts in this scene are stronger but you will notice that the tonal range is wider with darker darks though the highlights are no brighter. A wide ranger of blues is necessary, too, for the more complicated composition with greens for the foliage and glimpses of the weed in the water.

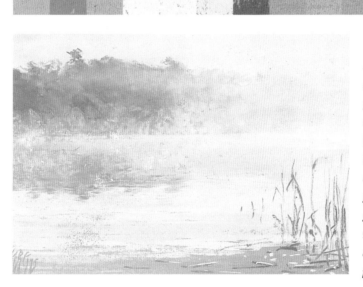

For this African swamp with the sun breaking through the mist, the palette is warm with, amongst others, pale tints of ultramarine blue, yellow ocher, sap green and burnt sienna, contrasted with some darker accents in raw umber, gray-green and cool gray. Pale scumbles give the impression of the mist rising from the water. Note how the colors are taken through from one part of the painting to the other.

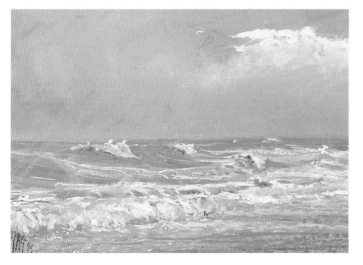

A stormy day blowing the tops off the waves is captured in a palette of blues of different tints with burnt umber, and some warm neutral grays for shadows and to give some contrast in temperature. The warm sandy color of the support is also an important "color" in the composition, showing through in all parts of the painting. Using fine grade sandpaper as a support lets the artist build up the white wate in areas of impasto.

Watercolor

Watercolors can be seen as a traditional medium for painting water, particularly rivers and streams where the watery landscapes and skies look like watercolor paintings before you even start. Yet a glimpse at examples in this book will show you how well this versatile medium travels, used expressively on pages 116–17 for salmon leaping the rapids, and for a coral cove on pages 138–9.

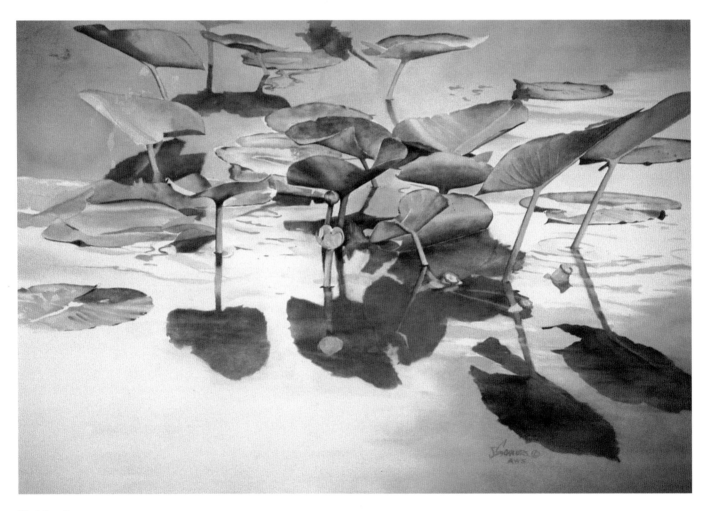

Golden Image
(watercolor)

JOHN SOWERS
Carefully building the image up from light to dark, the early washes are added wet-in-wet. Then darker, crisper-edged areas are added wet-on-dry.

If you want to add to the palette suggested on page 30, you might consider more greens if you are painting a river in a summer landscape – terre verte (a useful, earthy, gray-green), sap green (a bright yellow-green) and Hooker's green (a strong blue-green). Payne's gray, a blue-gray, is useful for mixing shadow colors although it can lead to rather boring shadows if used too much. Cerulean and cobalt blues are useful for painting the sea.

Painting water is never easy but the watercolor artist is truly tested when trying to capture fleeting light on water yet, when it works, it is magic. Laying a good wash is the essence of most watercolors and does take practice. Wait for areas to dry, or take out color with a rag or a brush loaded with water.

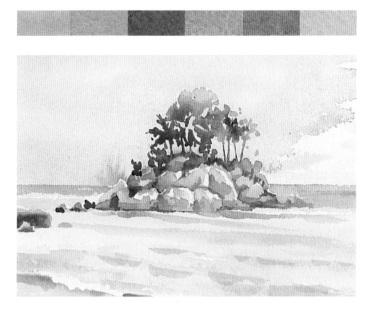

For this tropical sea a simple combination of ultramarine blue, cobalt blue and viridian green are used with the white surf reserved with liquid frisket so that it is simply the white of the paper. The darker area on the horizon and the waves are carefully built up with superimposed washes – wet-in-wet where the colors are to blend, and wet-on-dry where crisper edges are required. The vegetation on the island is equally simply developed with varying washes of Hooker's green, cadmium yellow, ultramarine blue and touches from the rock mix.

A combination of reality and imagination, this view of the Taj Mahal is built up in delicate superimposed washes, with the artist feeling intuitively for a mood. The warm resonance of the scene is set with an initial overall wash of aurora yellow with a touch of cadmium orange; then the water is built up with washes added and then smoothed and coaxed into position with a dry brush, keeping the strokes horizontal over the area of water. Any hard edges are taken back with clean water.

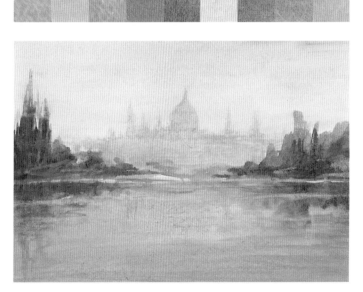

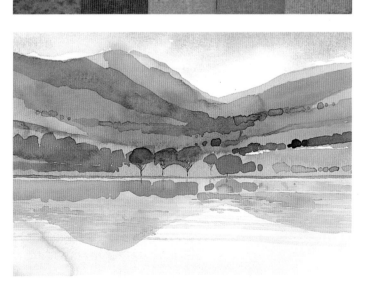

In this sketch of a view across a lake, the mountains in the distance are reflected as well as the closer line of trees. For the water, an initial wash of cobalt blue, with a little sap green and Payne's gray is superimposed with less dilute washes of the same mix for the mountains and a greener version for trees, applied wet-on-dry so that the outlines are clear. The horizontal lines across the area of water establish the plane and distinguish it from the real scene above.

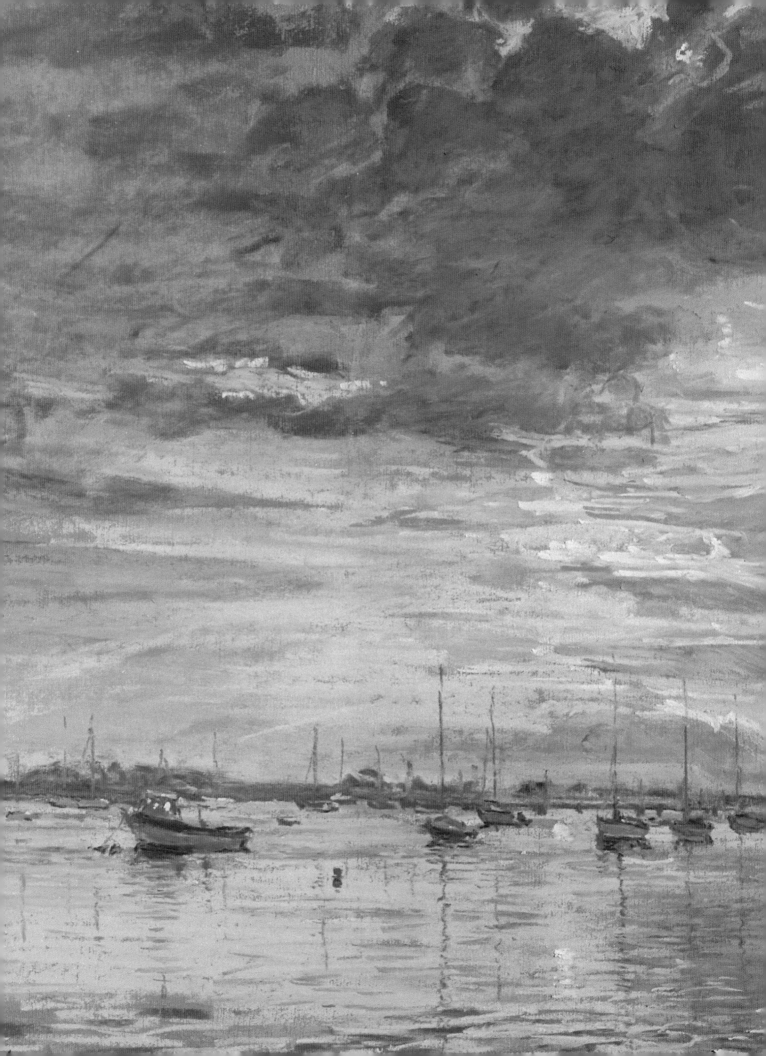

CHAPTER TWO

Still Water

To start with you may find it easier to try painting still water where the surface is flat and unaffected by winds and currents. Any sketching you can do at the side of a lake, pond or mere will help. When you have considered the necessary ingredients – reflections of the landscape and sky, shadows, the depth and "color" of the water, and those touches of reflected light – and pulled them together in your painting, suddenly you will have painted what appears to be water.

Sundown, Rambholt (pastel)
MARGARET GLASS
*In the still evening, when the wind has died, a
glorious sunset is reflected in the water in subtle
shades of yellow and pink.*

Still water

When we imagine still water, we tend to think of inland water: enclosed, sheltered areas such as duck ponds; lakes small enough to be surrounded by woods; or stagnant canals set below ground level. Yet vast lakes and lochs, lazy summer rivers, and even the sea, can be as flat as the proverbial millpond, particularly in the evening when the wind drops. Distance has the effect of smoothing out water, too, so large expanses can *appear* calm even when they are not.

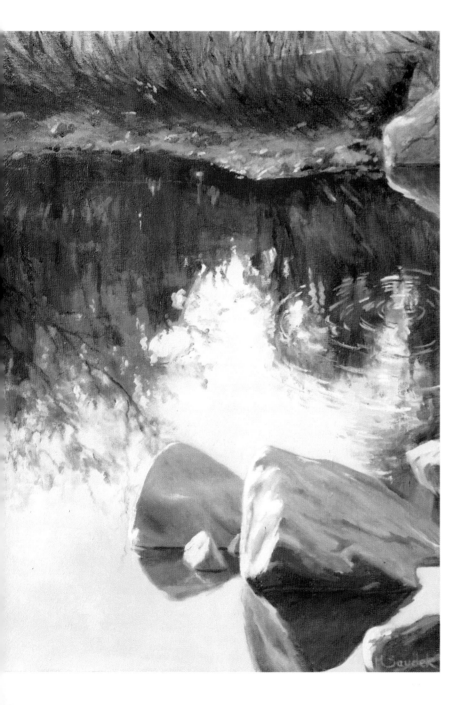

The factor common to all stretches of still water is that, because the surface is smooth and flat, it reflects everything around – and on – the water. Sky, buildings, trees, boats – all are pictured, mirror-like, on the surface. Yet still water also has depth. In some cases it is possible to see plants or pebbles on the bottom, or areas of sunlit sand. At other times you look down into a transparent darkness that seems to be unfathomable.

Observing water

From the artist's point of view, the appearance of any stretch of water is dictated by the weather, the season, the time of day and the landscape surrounding it. For this reason, every situation is different, and it is important to learn to observe water objectively – as a jigsaw of colors and patterns made up of reflections, shadows and fragments of light – and to analyze it in terms of light and dark tones and warm and cool colors set against each other.

Transparency and depth can be contrasted with opaque areas on the surface caused by reflections, surface plants and so

◀ **Evening Solitude** (oil)
MARTHA SAUDEK
Reflections and shadows are used to map out the surface of this still pool, while the concentric ripples establish the surface as two-dimensional.

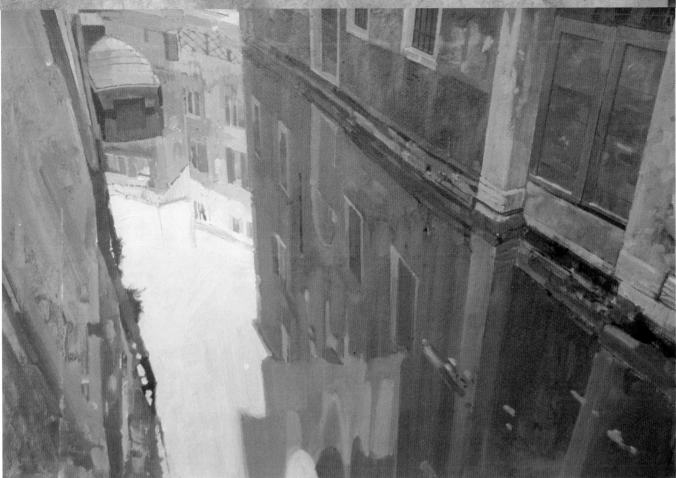

▲ **Reflections** (oil)

PETER KELLY

The artist uses the paint thinly for the reflections, but builds it up by superimposing more layers of paint for the surrounding architecture.

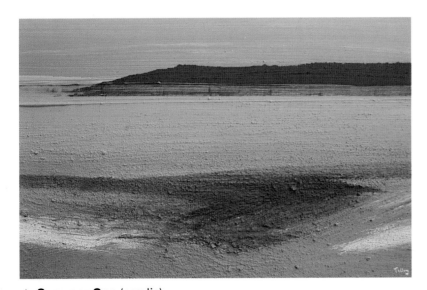

▲ **Summer Sea** (acrylic)

ROBERT TILLING

In the dying evening light a calm sea is given texture by addition of sand into the paint, more being added in the foreground than in the distance.

on. If you view water in this way, you will find it much easier to make sense of what you see, and to simplify and distil the important features in a scene into a few brushstrokes.

Analyzing mood

Still water, captured in a pond for example, may at first seem an easier option to paint than waves, which are three-dimensional as well as constantly on the move. But it is always tricky to put across the transparent, reflective, and, in places, infinitely deep quality of still water. It helps to have an understanding of why the light catches the water in a certain way or why you can see into the water in some places and not in others.

When looking at a stretch of still water that you want to paint, you need to analyze its "color," mood, depth, reflections, and shadows. In time these considerations become automatic, computed with a single glance, but the less experienced artist needs to gather and assess the relevant information in a more conscious way.

Photo ideas

Photographs can help you to look at a view objectively, as if looking at it in a mirror. They can also act as a trigger to the imagination. Here are some different views of still waters to give you some ideas.

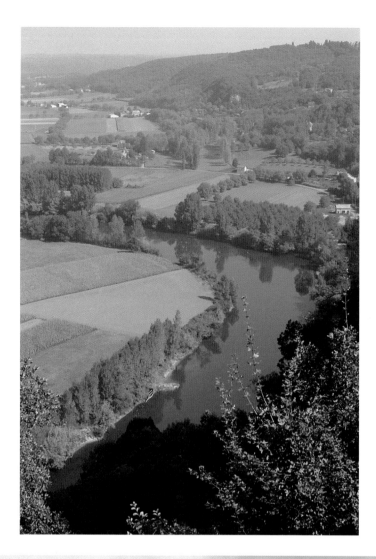

▶ **The Dordogne, France**
Seen from a bird's eye view, this majestic river carves through the landscape, reflecting the sky and surrounding trees.

▶ **Wast Water, Lake District, England**
The mountains are reflected in the still water but note how the outlines are broken, the colors muted, and tones darker. In the foreground you can see the stones on the lake bed which would be worth bringing out.

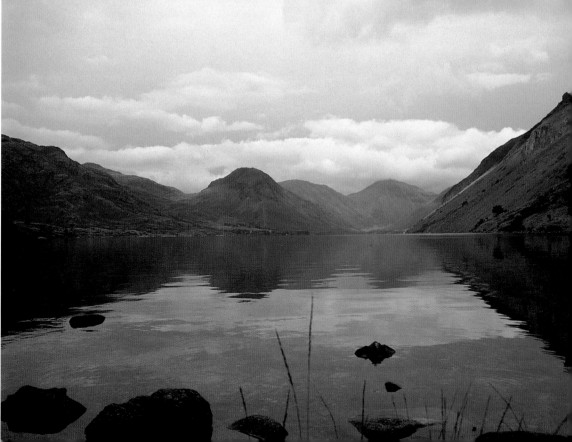

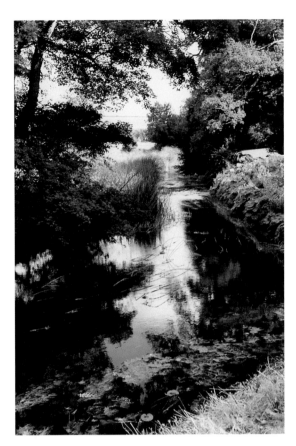

◀ **The River Cherwell at Rousham, Oxfordshire, England**
In a shaded backwater, the shadows appear dark in sharp contrast with the reflections of the sky.

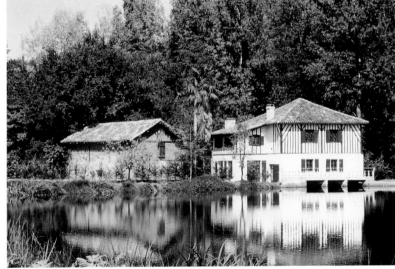

▲ **Lake Houses**
You will need to make the bright reflections darker than in the photograph or the eye will be confused.

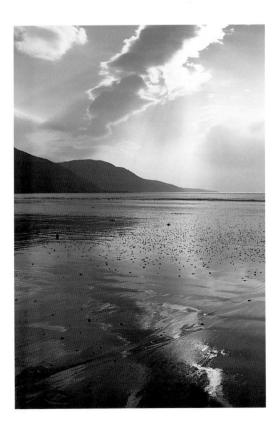

◀ **Wet Sands**
In the weak evening light, the reflection of the headland is barely perceptible on the slightly ruffled sea but is very clear on the wet sand.

The color of water

To talk about the color of water is meaningless. Although a body of water appears to have a color, it will never appear as one flat color. What you see as the "color" of the water is created by reflections of everything around it. Indeed, you have to train yourself to see the water not as one color, but as an area of different, interlocking colors.

It is helpful to treat water as having an underlying color, which you can lay down or block in, early on, as a wash to provide a tonal and color key for the rest of the painting. Children tend to paint all water blue, yet streams sometimes contain peaty water, which is reddish-brown, lakes can show a myriad of greens, and the sea all colors from bright turquoise in a tropical coral cove to a deep murky brown on a stormy day in the English Channel. This underlying color is affected by such diverse influences as the depth of the water,

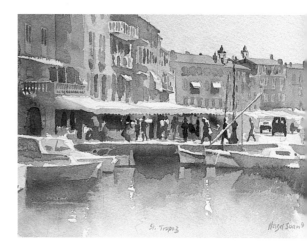

◄ **Alonissos Boat** (watercolor)
BRYN CRAIG
The colors of the water have been painted mainly wet-in-wet, with some areas of wet-on-dry to give them crisper edges.

Laying a Watercolor Wash

The underlying color of this inlet of sea water is blue because it reflects the sky, but as the water varies in depth, it is not a solid blue. In addition, although the water appears flat when seen from a distance, it has some movement. Because these details are not clearly visible from a distance, the artist hints at them by varying the intensity of the wash.

◀ **Summer Heat, St Tropez**
(watercolor)
HAZEL SOAN
The underlying color of the water comes from the yellow light. Shadows are superimposed.

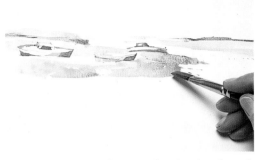

1 *First paint in the boats with a fine brush, and then wash in the sand color around them.*

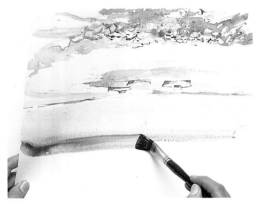

2 *Turn the paper upside down and hold it in a vertical position. Wash in the sky adding more color as you work down the paper to give the idea of the sky receding towards the horizon. Turn the paper the right way up again to create interesting backruns.*

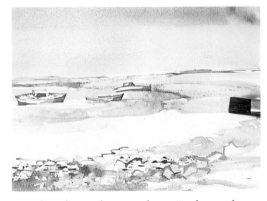

3 *When the sand area is dry, mix plenty of dilute blue and quickly wash in the sea color using a large brush, taking the color over the edge of the sand. Vary the intensity of color in the wash and remember that it will dry paler.*

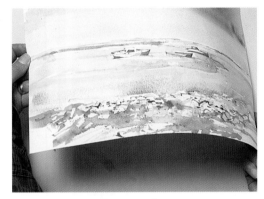

4 *By bending and tipping the paper, you can control the direction in which the wash spreads. Here the artist breaks up the wash. Heavy watercolor paper, which need not be stretched, can be handled in this way without cockling.*

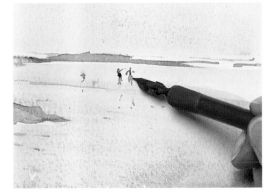

5 *Using a pen and dilute watercolor (use a small brush to load the nib with paint), add in some small figures on the far shore for interest and to set the scale. Note how the sea wash has granulated, giving it an attractive texture.*

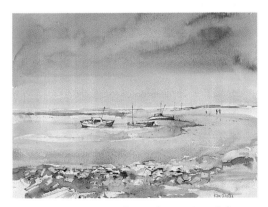

6 *The variation in color and intensity of the wash used for the sea captures the changing color of the water, caused by variable factors such as shallows and turbulence.*

Building up Color and Tone

This painting on a colored ground is built up in stages by superimposing one thin, broken layer of color over another. Acrylics are opaque and dry quickly, so have a good choice. Scumbled highlights are added at the end with pastels.

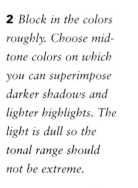

1 *Apply a yellow ocher ground with a coarse brush, sweeping the paint in all directions. Glimpses of this layer will be visible in the final painting, giving unity and light.*

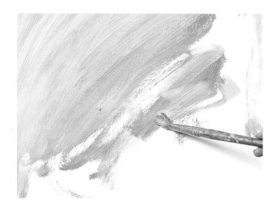

2 *Block in the colors roughly. Choose mid-tone colors on which you can superimpose darker shadows and lighter highlights. The light is dull so the tonal range should not be extreme.*

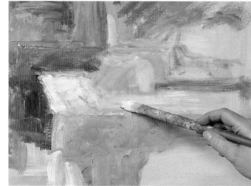

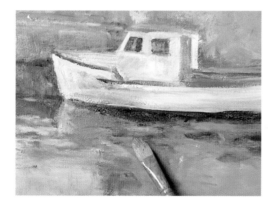

3 *Build up the reflections in dull blues and greens, letting the paint underneath show in places. Murky green lightly applied with dryish paint creates a smoky layer.*

4 *Having built up the darker tones, use pale pastel chalks on their sides to scumble highlights over the water. The texture of the paper and rough paint will break up the pastel strokes.*

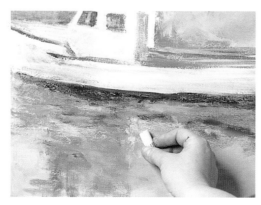

suspended particles, changes in the make-up of the river or sea bed, the sky, and the quality of the light. The turquoise of a coral cove, for example, is a combination of sunlight, clear water, reflections of the blue sky above and the golden, sandy sea bed below. This combination of influences also demonstrates that, even though you need to assess the main color of a body of water, water is never a single, flat color.

Color and depth

The appearance of a stretch of water varies according to its depth, the intensity of the underlying color increasing where the water is deeper. In shallower water, the color is affected by the sun reflecting off the bottom – yellow where it is sandy, warm browns where there are dark, muddy depths, and greenish where there are weeds.

If you stand by the side of a lake, you are presented with clues as to how deep the water is. Can you see the bottom? If not, the

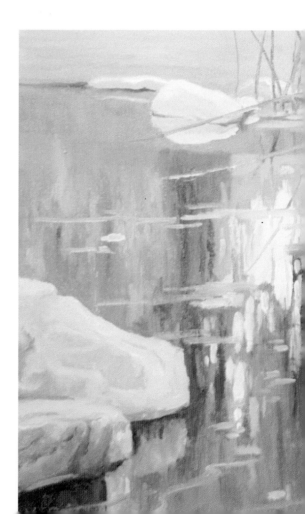

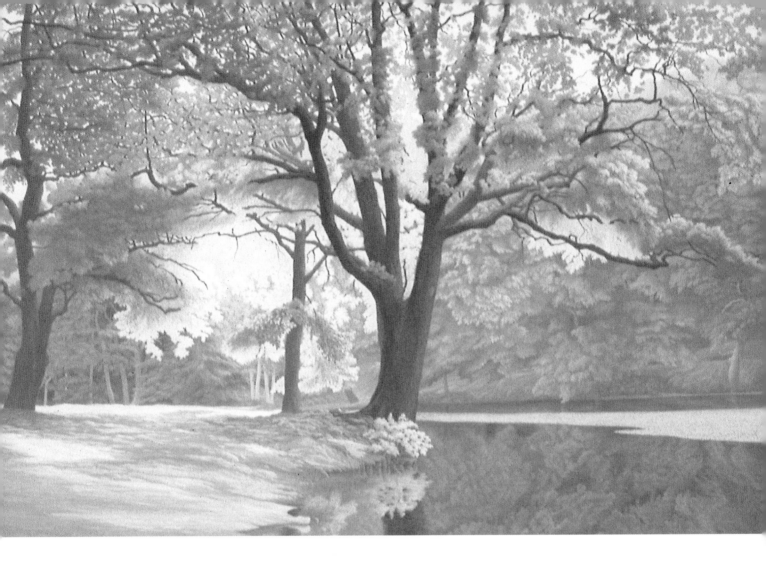

water is murky or deep, which will probably call for a dark overall color. Water that is almost black suggests infinite, foreboding depths. Of course the quality of the light will affect your perception of the color. In dull light, the water will appear darker and it will be difficult to see below the surface. In brighter light, the varying depths will be easier to see.

If you are using opaque paints, or pastels, lay the dark, underlying color down first and superimpose lighter reflections over the top. Alternatively, with pastels, you could work on a dark paper, using the background color for the darkest areas. With watercolor, you

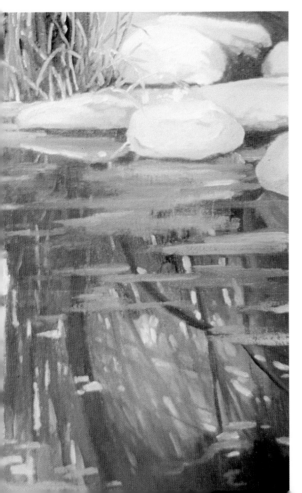

◀ **Secluded Pond** (oil)

MARTHA SAUDEK

Although the reflections of the bankside vegetation predominate, the placing of surface plants next to shadow areas provides hints of foreboding depths in the water.

▲ **Waggoners' Wells** (gouache)

JEAN CANTER

In the water area dark washes are applied wet-on-dry over lighter green ones, and the reflections are then lifted out with paper towels wrapped around the brush end.

Wet-in-Wet Watercolor over Masked-out Highlights

For the indefinable depths of this city riverscape, the water is painted with a combination of murky blues and greens fed wet-in-wet-style over reserved highlights.

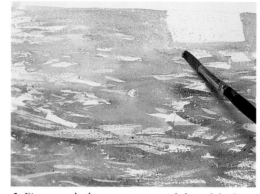

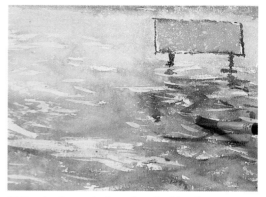

1 *First streak the water area with liquid frisket. You can try flicking it, too, to break up the paint surface in the background. When the liquid frisket is dry, mix a gray wash and brush it over the area unevenly, adding touches of blue and green into the wet wash.*

2 *Put in the noticeboard and add ocher reflections of it in the water below, first wetting the paper with clean water so that the colors bleed into each other without any hard edges.*

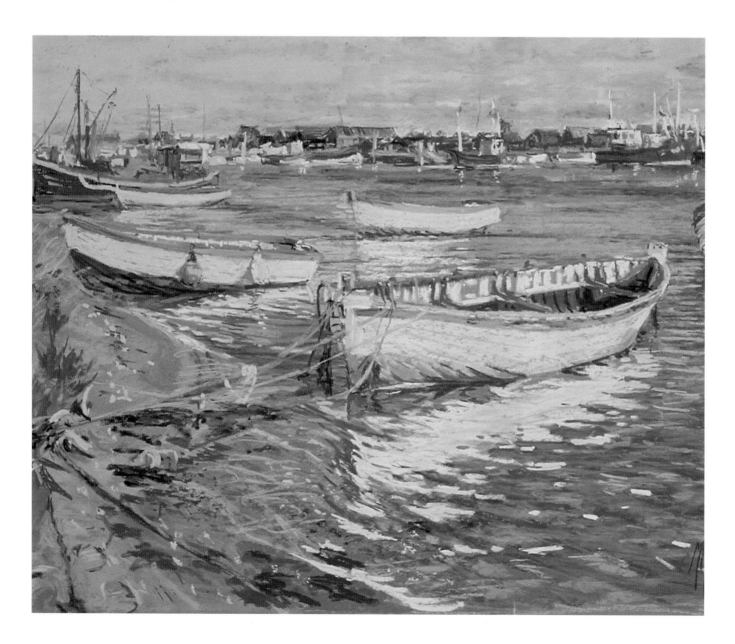

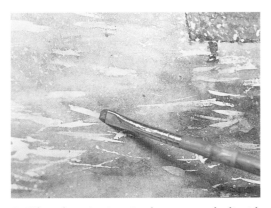

3 *When the paint is quite dry, remove the liquid frisket by rubbing it with a clean finger. At this point you may want to knock back any white highlights that are too bright with a transparent gray wash.*

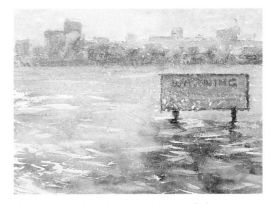

4 *Having added the city skyline and the smog-filled sky, you can see how this combination of techniques successfully suggest indefinable murky depths.*

can isolate the highlights with liquid frisket and then build up a tremendous depth of tone with superimposed washes to hint at the murky depths. With oils a very effective way to create an impression of receding depth is to use color glazes. Use transparent colors, and glaze them over the top of each other rather than mixing them first. If you are working in oils and using transparent colors for the water, remember that you can vary the intensity of the color just by varying the thickness of the paint. You don't need to mix in white to modify a color for less intense areas, for example where the water is shallower, just apply the paint more thinly there than in areas where you want to suggest more depth.

Where you can see the bottom of a lake or pond, don't try to be too literal about the details. It is best represented with a suggestion of forms and colors on the bottom set against reflections, plants or whatever on the surface.

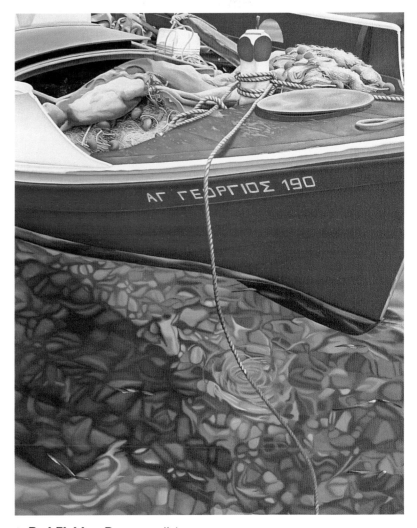

◀ **Tied up, Walberswick** (pastel)

MARGARET GLASS

A mid-brown tinted paper is used to represent the sandy seabed, and reflections of the sky and boat have been scumbled over the top.

▲ **Red Fishing Boat** (acrylic)

NICK HARRIS

If you look down into clear blue water, you can see refracted light as a mosaic of shapes.

Reflections

Wetness and reflectivity are two qualities that make water different from other natural phenomena. To capture these qualities in a manner that creates an illusion of water, you need to forget that an area of water is a continuous surface to be treated in a consistent manner, and see it only as existing through its surroundings. Water is the sky above the trees and houses around, the sands and rock below, and the handful of swimmers in it.

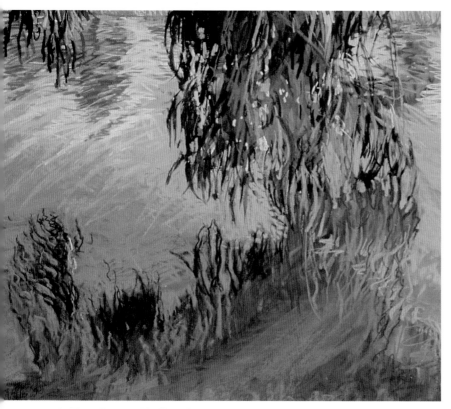

▲ **Eucalyptus Reflections**
(pastel over watercolor underpainting)
KITTY WALLIS
This is painted on fine sandpaper to give a surface that takes the pastels well. The sky reflections are built up from dark to light with intuitive, dancing strokes that capture the heat and light.

The ways in which you apply the paint for an object and its reflection determine whether the viewer reads this patchwork of shapes and colors as water or as something solid. The reflections also show the state of the water: whether it is calm or rough, rippling or surging. And the state of the water, in turn, conveys the mood of the painting.

Reflections of the sky

On an open piece of water, reflections of the sky often dominate the color of the water. Such reflections, however, are rarely true to the sky color, but tend to reflect a general overall color, even when clouds are clearly articulated. In most conditions reflections of the sky, therefore, are generalized and simplified, and require a broad treatment in paint.

Even when the water appears flat and still, reflections of the sky will lack detail and be slightly distorted, like the reflection in an old mirror. If you do paint the reflection exactly like the sky, the eye is confused and jumps from sky to water, trying to work out what, precisely, is going on. Therefore you have to give the eye a clue that there is sky in the upper part of the painting and the reflection of the sky in the water by generalizing the reflection more than is the case in reality.

If you take time to study reflections, you will notice that the colors are not always true to the object casting them, but tend to be modified by the "color" of the body of water. Again, even if, to you, the colors of object and reflection look the same, it will not work to paint them that way. The artist has to exaggerate the difference in color between the sky and its reflection so that the viewer can see a difference.

Techniques for sky reflections

Sky reflections must be treated in a way that hints at the horizontal plane of the water. You can think of it as trying to capture the three-dimensional nature of the clouds themselves with techniques that suit them, and treating the reflections of the clouds in the water as two-dimensional and opaque. Apply opaque paints in a way that emphasizes the two-dimensional surface of the water, laying the paint on in broad, sweeping strokes, treating the clouds as large, overall shapes, and ignoring detail. Watercolor washes produce the same sense of the two-dimensional.

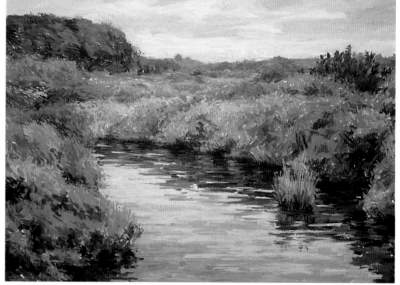

▲ **Pamet River in Summer** (pastel)
SIMIE MARYLES
Reflections of the sky are mapped out on the surface plane of the water using regular, parallel strokes.

▼ **Lakeside, Italy** (watercolor)
PAUL KENNY
The setting sun creates a luminous reflection built up with superimposed washes.

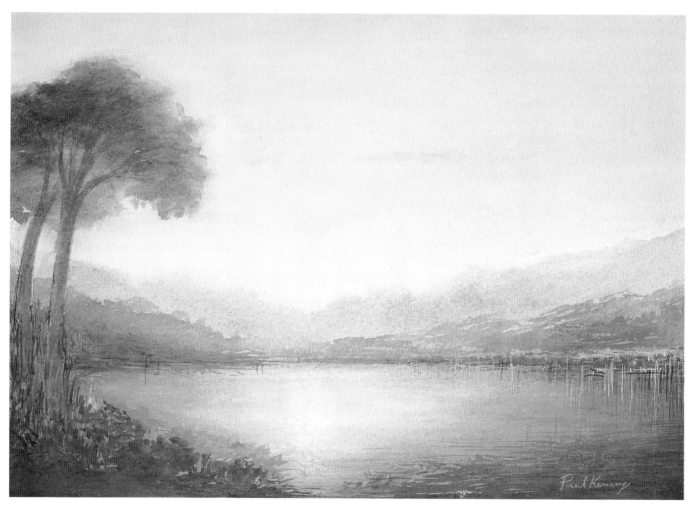

For a reflection to exist, there has to be light, and the quality of the light will affect the reflection: the stronger the light, the more intense the reflection will be. You will have seen how dazzling a stretch of water can be on a bright but cloudy day, when the water reflects back the overall whiteness of the cloud cover. On dull days when the light is weak, a cloudy sky will not dominate the water in the same way.

On the horizon

There is a particular problem when the sky meets water on the horizon. You might imagine that with the sky reflected in the sea, they would be very similar in tone. Observation reveals, however, that the sea, or a lake, will always be darker in tone, whatever the state of the sky. You can differentiate between sky and water by knocking back the sky color, or you can treat the two areas with different techniques.

If you are using watercolor, you can paint the sky wet-in-wet, letting the colors fuse together, and paint the water with flat, superimposed washes. With opaque media,

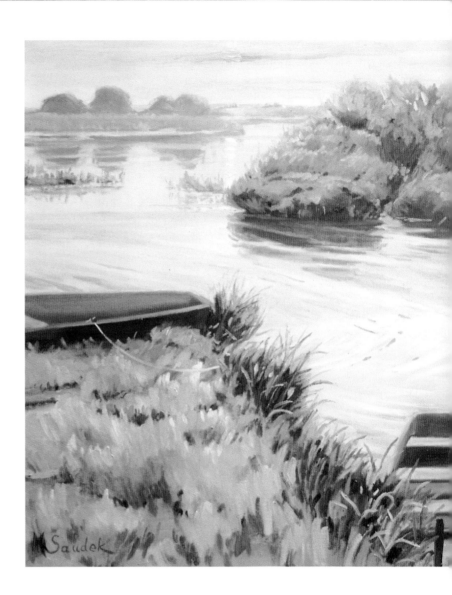

Colored Ground Uniting Sky and Water

A simple way to create a reflection of the sky in the water below is by first coloring the whole surface with a mid-tone sky color. Then work from that mid-tone above and below the horizon.

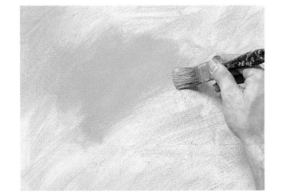

1 *On canvas board, first cover the ground with a dilute acrylic, mid-tone blue-gray. Use a large, soft brush and work the paint over the canvas with uneven strokes. Once dry, add another layer.*

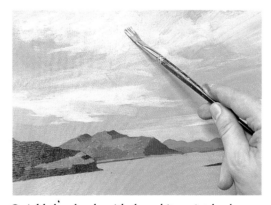

2 *Add the clouds with dry white paint broken with a touch of the mid-tone gray, working thinly over the ground with a gentle scrubbing motion.*

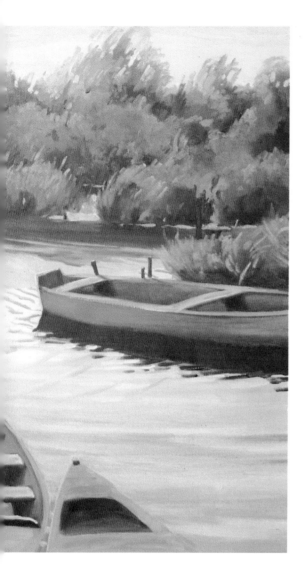

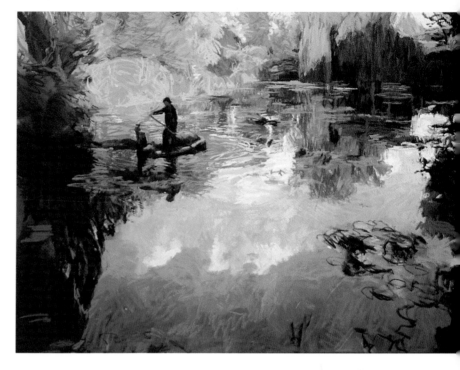

◀ **Brittany's La Brière I** (oil)
MARTHA SAUDEK
Soft reflections are created by working with a limited range of blue tones and blending them with the soft yellow of the evening light.

▲ **Mowing the Pond** (pastel over acrylic wash)
KITTY WALLIS
In the cold blue light of early morning, extreme contrasts between light and dark and vibrant sky reflections jostle the eye until it focuses on the lone mower.

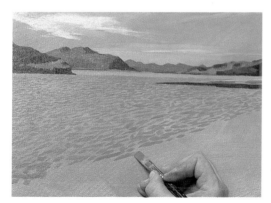

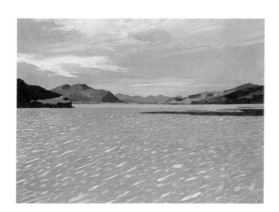

3 *Add the ripples on the water in a darker version of the original blue-gray. Dab the paint on with brushstrokes that get smaller and closer together in the distance, and let the base color show through in places. Add the highlights last.*

4 *With the highlights added in dilute white, so that it is qualified by the strokes beneath, the painting comes to life.*

Deepening the Color on the Horizon

Looking out to sea, you will notice that the color often intensifies towards the horizon. Here the canvas board is divided into three sections: sand, sea and sky, and the deep blue of the sea is gradually built up as the painting progresses.

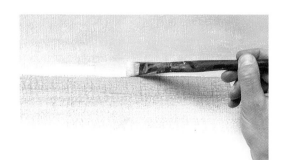

1 *Keeping the acrylic paint dilute, block in the sea and then the sky, bringing the sky down to the horizon and slightly blending it with the sea color.*

you can handle the sky in a lively fashion, laying down color with fresh, varied brush-strokes, and put in the sea with broader, flatter strokes. For oils or acrylics, you could apply the paint with a knife in the sea area. Another approach is to change the direction of the brushwork, using horizontal strokes for the sky and vertical ones for the water. Pastels lend themselves to this treatment.

Never paint a line at the horizon. Merge the sky and water tones into each other so that there isn't a strong contrast there, which would work against any sense of distance in the painting, and so that sky and sea on the horizon are equally far back in space. On large areas of water, you may have noticed that the color seems to deepen on the horizon. This natural phenomenon helps to delineate between sky and water but should not be exaggerated.

2 *Build up the sky in uneven layers of paint. Darken the sea toward the horizon with steady, horizontal strokes, keeping the paint thin. Add a pale yellow, flat wash to the foreground.*

Landscape reflections

Reflections of the surrounding landscape, and of any objects on the water surface, have two particularly important characteristics. Wherever you are standing, reflections are always directly below the object casting them and appear to extend across the water surface toward you. So, if you move from side to side, they seem to follow you. Secondly, because they are caused by light being reflected off the surface of the water, they are opaque, and this provides a good clue to painting them.

Another important feature of reflections is that when you are facing an object close to the water's edge, the reflection of that object extends from its base, not from the edge of the water. If the object, such as a tree or

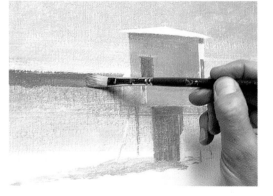

3 *Having added the tower, intensify the sea colors. Apply the paint with parallel strokes to enforce the horizontal plane of the water. Blur the edge along the horizon with a finger or a clean rag.*

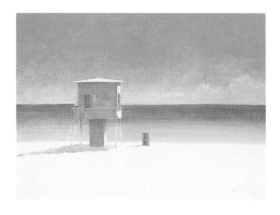

4 *A rusting red barrel adds focus, representing the viewer staring out to sea. The daring depth of blue on the horizon gives the impression of infinite distance on a hot, clear day.*

building, is set back from the water's edge – even only a short way – you will not see the bottom of it reflected in the water. How much is included in the reflection is in direct relation to the distance that the object reflected is set back from the water. So in any scene observe carefully how much is included in the reflections.

Even when water appears to be glass-like in its stillness, it is rarely so in actuality as reflections will show you. There is always a slight movement in the water that distorts, blurs and elongates the image of the harbor houses or the coppice of trees; or a breath of wind that fragments the reflected image. In the same way, reflections are never quite the same colors as the objects that reflect them. Colors are generally muted, as if seen over distance. Reflections of dark green trees will be weaker in tone than the actual trees and the color will be less saturated, while a white house or boat will appear darker in tone.

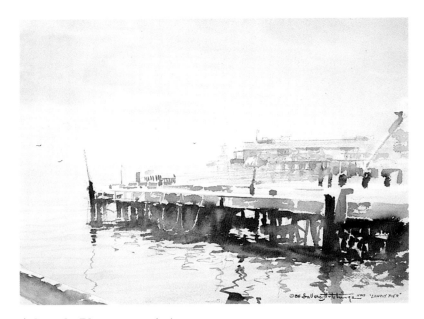

▲ **Lonely Pier** (watercolor)

LaVere Hutchings

For a haunting misty horizon, let the sky and the sea blend.

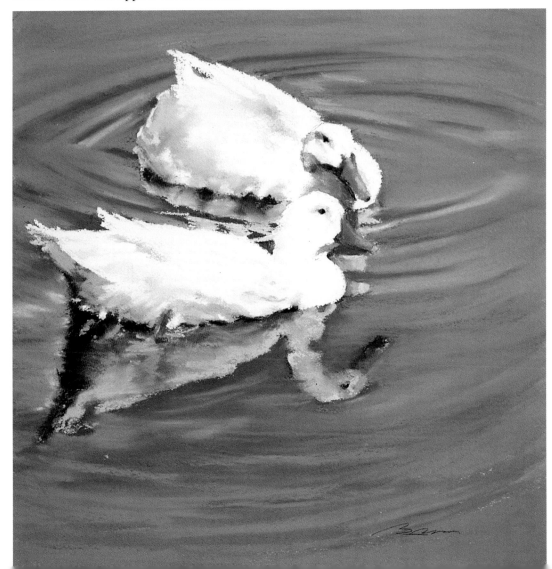

◀ **Inlet Circles** (pastel)

Jann T. Bass

Although the water appears glass-like, the reflections of these ducks appear distorted in shape and outline, with muted colors and darker in tone.

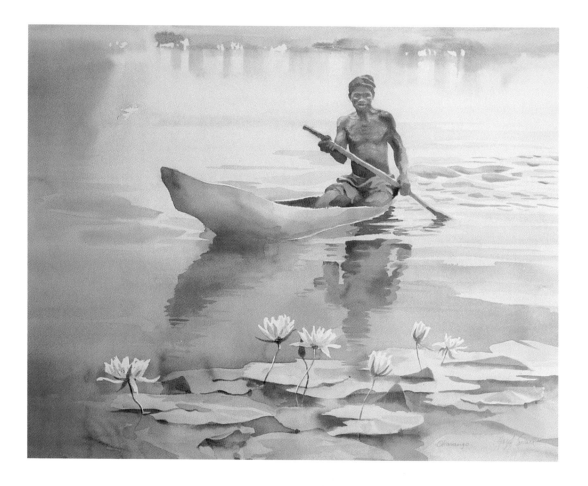

◄ **Mokoro**
(watercolor)
HAZEL SOAN
*Reflections on water
come toward the
viewer. They can be
worked out by
dropping verticals
from the objects and
measuring distances
above and below the
water level.*

▼ **The Wingfield
Castle before
Restoration**
(watercolor)
STEPHEN CROWTHER
*The reflection looks
darker in tone than
the ship and is
distorted by the
movement in the
water.*

Perspective and reflections

When you are trying to work out reflections
in a painting away from the subject, imagine
the water as a mirror set at right angles to
the object you are painting. All vertical lines
in the object continue for the same distance
in the reflected image on the water. Receding
planes above water are reflected identically
with horizontal lines converging on the same
vanishing point as those of the object itself.
Even when looking at boats from an odd
angle or a tree trunk that is half submerged,
you can plot the reflections by dropping the
verticals and measuring the distance above
and below the water level.

You can study the way reflections work
by using a mirror. Place it flat on a table or
on the floor and arrange some objects close
to the edge. Now move the mirror around
and see how the reflections are affected by
changes in your viewpoint and eye level.
Look at it from above and on the level, from
the left and from the right. You will see how

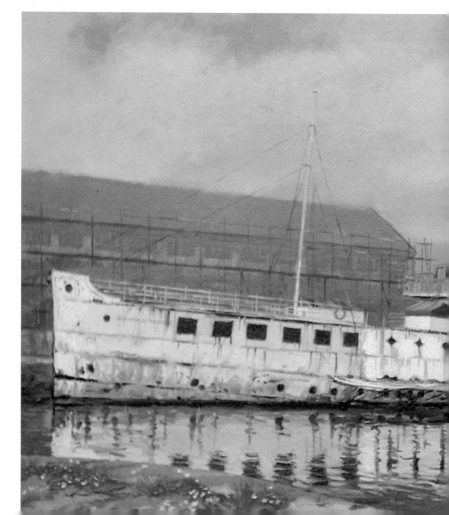

the reflection always points toward you. When you view objects face on at water level, perspective has little effect, and similarly so in the reflection. When you view objects from above, however, they will appear fore-shortened, as will the reflection. Seen obliquely, receding planes will be mirrored in the water. Any effects of perspective that you see in the object will be reflected in the water.

You can see what happens when the water is disturbed by a breeze if you spray the mirror with a clear spray cleaner. The reflected image is then considerably reduced in clarity, with loss of detail and a reduction in the strength of the colors.

Studying reflections

The balance of tones and colors is constantly changing, so study reflections in different conditions and at different times of day. Colors do not always behave as theory dictates. Sometimes mid-tone colors – even whole buildings – hardly reflect at all and

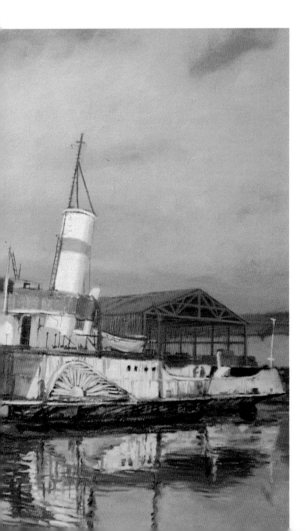

Painting Reflections

Using opaque paints, here acrylics on heavy watercolor paper, you can lay in the darker areas of reflections first and then work the highlights over the top. The grainy paper breaks up the paint so the previous layers show through.

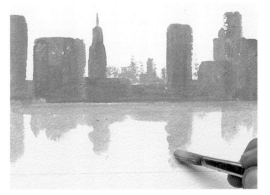

1 *Block in the New York skyline with a dark gray, adding the paler reflection below. Make the reflections imprecise, using interlocking horizontal strokes.*

2 *Paint in the pinkish evening sky, and work a more dilute version of this color around the reflections. Overlap the sky reflections over those of the buildings in places.*

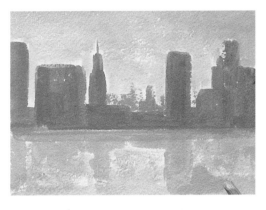

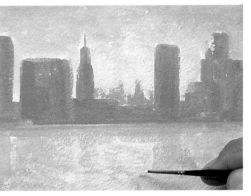

3 *To establish the water area, add white to the pinkish tint and dab the paint over the area with a small brush, smudging some strokes with a finger to spread the paint.*

4 *Finally, add lights and their reflections across the water with white tinted with yellow. Touch on the paint following a dancing path, and make it less distinct away from the source.*

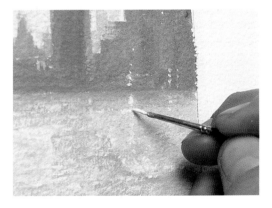

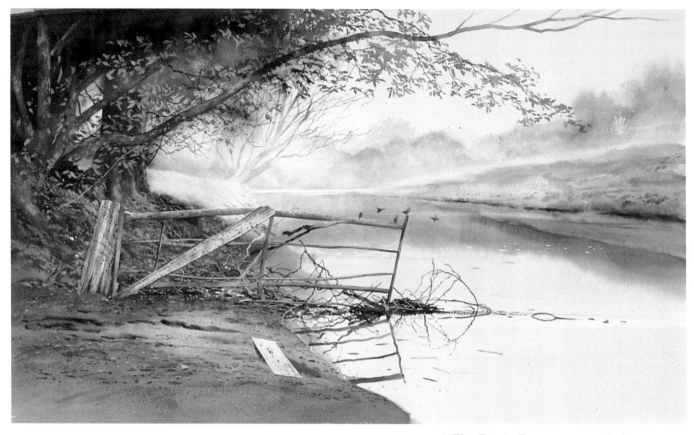

▲ **The Rusty Fence** (watercolor)
RICHARD BOLTON
Although misty, the light is bright, and reflections in the foreground are clearer than those in the distance.

some dark colors can look even darker in the reflection. In a lake in a park, for example, you may see parts of a waterside building show up as a blurred patch, whereas others shine brightly and clearly. In practice, this gives the artist a certain amount of license in manipulating the tonal values to suit the composition.

Breaking up the reflection

Any movement on the surface of the water – maybe a swell, or ruffles and ripples caused by a breeze breaking the surface – will break up reflections to some degree from slight distortion to the complete fragmentation of the reflected image. Reflections of masts appear to snake their way across the water, and the edges of roofs and boats will take on this irregularity as well. Reflections are generally harder edged where they are close to the subject, the edges becoming more diffused and broken up as they get farther away.

Breaking up reflections takes patience and keen observation, but by painting them fragmented and distorted by the movement

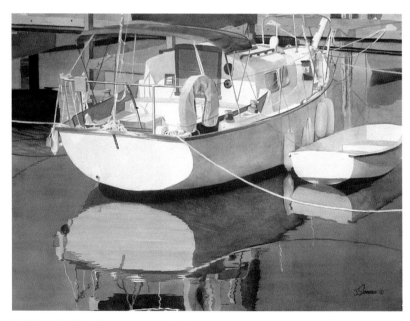

▲ **Blue Reflection** (watercolor)
JOHN SOWERS
The apparently glass-like water still distorts the reflected image in shape, color and outline.

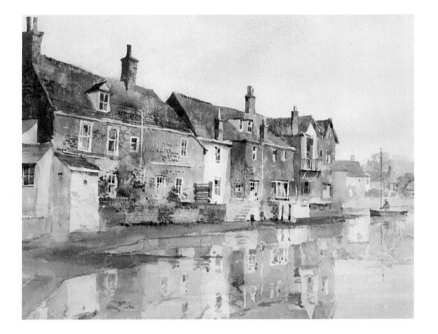

◀ **Bosham Reflections** (watercolor)

Tom Groom

In weak light, the reflections are subdued in tone, built up with delicate wet-on-dry washes.

of the water, and weaker in color than the surroundings, you will be halfway to creating the illusion of water. Most problems arise where the reflection is painted too literally, with colors and tones too strong. Keep the paint thin and flat to emphasize the two-dimensional nature of the reflection and to contrast it with the more plastic reality on shore.

Techniques for reflections

As with skies, reflections of the surroundings have to be treated in a different way to the surroundings themselves so that the viewer can tell what is what. Generally, treat reflections more broadly, using more generalized, less detailed strokes, and blur the edges increasingly the farther the reflection is from the object casting it.

With watercolor, reflections that constitute the darkest areas of the water will be added last, over the colors of the rest of the

Using Turpentine with Oil Pastels

Light shines on a pool of water through a thick canopy of trees, creating stark contrasts between light and dark in a limited range of colors. The water is given a fluid surface by using turpentine to blend the pastel strokes.

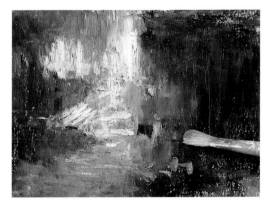

1 *Map out the tones with lively hatched strokes. The warm-toned paper and browny reds will show through in the final picture as points of warm light.*

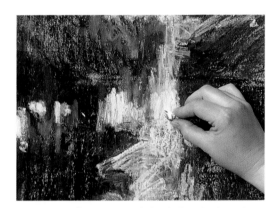

2 *Build up the still water by working greens and sky reflections into the tonal underdrawing, and then paint turpentine into the water area to blend the pastel strokes.*

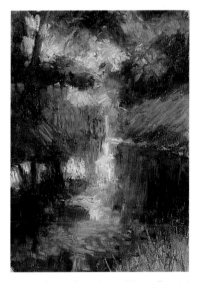

3 *Break up the mirror-like reflectivity of the pool with patches of weed in the foreground made with abrupt strokes of pale green. The result is mysterious and atmospheric.*

water, wet-on-dry. Work up the lighter reflections first, and add the darker areas around them. Masts and other delicate reflections crossing a large area of water can be reserved at the beginning with liquid frisket so that the wash going on for the water does not need to be interrupted.

With oils and acrylics, you could try using a larger brush to paint the reflection for broader approach. Reflections are best painted with vertical brushstrokes, rather than horizontal ones. Avoid applying the paint with wiggly brushstrokes, but you can distort the reflected image by wiggling a dry brush through the applied paint. With pastels, you could try using the side of the chalk to create the reflection, which will force you to keep the image loose and make it difficult to add too many details.

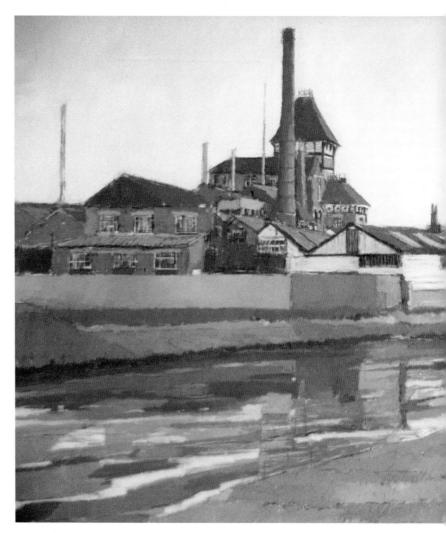

▲ **Harvey's Brewery, Lewis** (oil)
NICK BREMER
The complicated architecture of the bank is reflected in broad shapes in the river.

Superimposing a Light Reflection over a Darker Body Color

Using acrylic paints on watercolor paper, the underlying color of the water is established first, and the broken reflection is worked over the top with small, horizontal strokes.

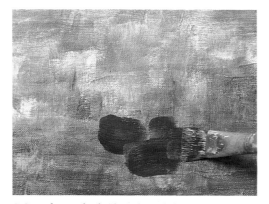

1 *Lay down the body color of the water using a coarse, square brush to make block-like interlocking strokes – apply a pale layer first, and then a darker one. Let the paper show through in places.*

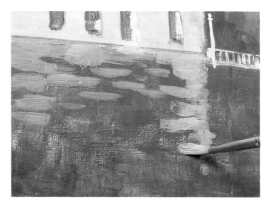

2 *Use the color of the buildings in the reflections, but let the blue merge with it and dull it. Lay in the reflections with horizontal strokes of dry paint, imitating the slightly broken water.*

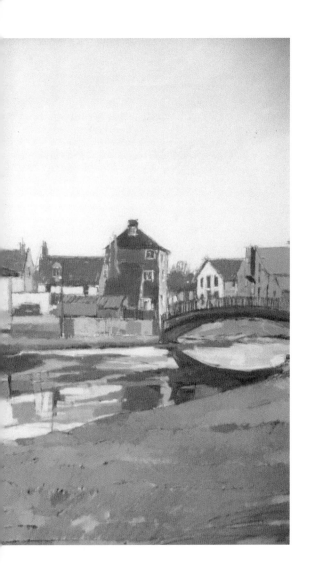

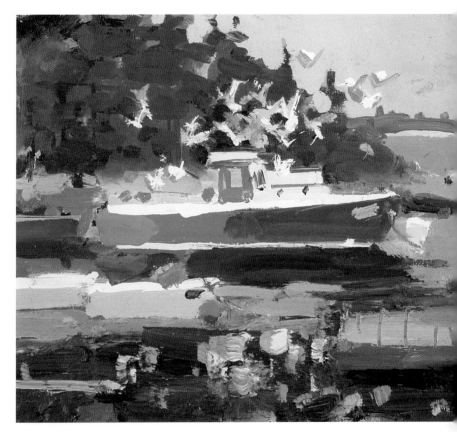

▲ **Gulls and Boat, Maine** (oil)

CHARLES SOVEK

Oil paint can be used thickly and pushed around until the desired effect is achieved.

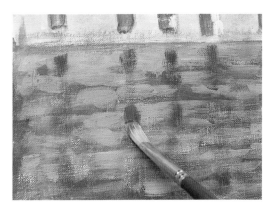

3 *Having built up the pale reflections with lighter applications, take a clean, dry brush and load it with a touch of the dark mix, removing the excess on a rag. Lightly drybrush over the pale strokes for the reflections of the windows.*

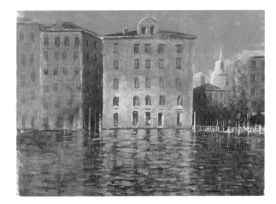

4 *Seen from a distance, the individual strokes merge and the reflection appears to dance on the gently ruffled water. Note how reflections are weaker and less distinct the farther they are from the objects being reflected.*

Shadows on the water

On any stretch of still water set in a landscape shadows and reflections will combine. The beauty of an area of shadow cast by trees or rocks onto still water is that it lets you see below the surface to undefined depths or to the stony bed of the lake or pond. Shadows therefore appear as an absence of reflection rather than the normal absence of light, giving the artist the opportunity for imaginative passages within the patchwork of reflections.

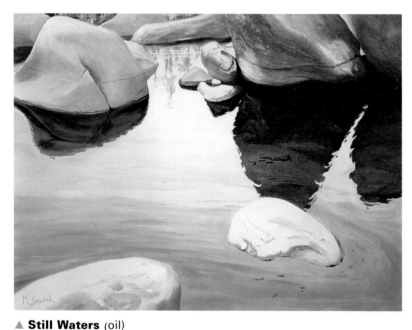

▲ **Still Waters** (oil)

MARTHA SAUDEK

Shadows of overhanging rocks interrupt the reflections on the surface, letting us see the pebbles underwater.

Shadows on water are like shadows anywhere else. They appear where the light rays from the sun are intercepted by elements of the landscape, such as trees, or objects on the water, such as boats, and they are affected by the quality and the position of that light and the reflectivity of the water. This means that weak light will cast pale shadows with indefinite edges, whereas shadows cast by strong light will be darker and more crisply defined. The position of the sun in the sky will also affect the shadows cast – low in the sky and the shadows will be long and weak such as in the early morning; at midday when the sun is high in the sky, they will be short and dark.

The state of the water itself will affect the shadows cast. If it is still, the shadow will be seen as an absence of reflection on the surface of the water, allowing the dark depths to be seen. Ripples or wavelets, however, will catch the light from the sky at an angle and the shadow will be lost.

Casting shadows

Shadows are cast away from the light. If you stand on the edge of a pond and look across at a large tree, as long as there is light in the sky the reflection of the tree will always come towards you. The shadow, though, is cast away from the light, only coming toward you if the tree is backlit.

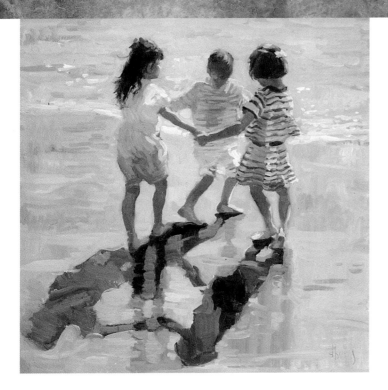

◄ **Shadow Dance** (oil)

DENISE BURNS

Here, with the light behind the children, the shadows are cast across the wet sand towards the viewer, raking to the left. The reflections are played down but are still there.

Building up the Shadow Wet-in-Wet and Wet-on-Dry

With watercolors, murky depths are described by merging colors wet-in-wet, while crisper edges come from washes superimposed wet-on-dry. With the light behind the boat, the shadow comes toward the viewer, and it is possible to see through it to the shadow cast by the boat on the sandy seabed below.

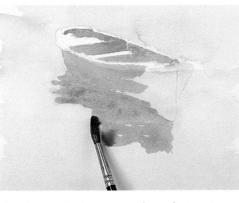

1 *Wash over the boat, apart from the interior, with pale yellow. When dry, add the shadow on the side of the boat and water, feeding it on unevenly to give a blotchy appearance.*

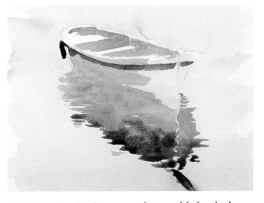

2 *Before the shadow area dries, add the darker shadow on the sea bed wet-in-wet so that the colors merge. Dab it over the dry yellow wash, too, for crisper edges.*

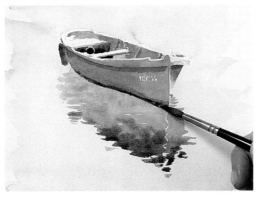

3 *Bring on the boat with tones of blue and a wash of gray. Before the paint is quite dry, add the water line. It should be neither too crisp nor run. Test with a small stroke first.*

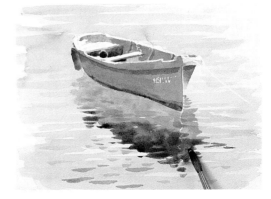

4 *To create the broken water surface, add a pale blue wash in streaky horizontal strokes over the yellow, darker in the foreground. Finally add a few touches of the darkest shadow.*

Remember with objects in the water, the shadow lets you see that object below the surface. If you watch a child paddling with the light behind her, you will see her reflection extending toward you; but where the shadow is cast, you will be able to see her legs under water. Similarly, a boat will cast a shadow in the reflection of the hull.

Perspective and shadows

You will need to apply the rules of perspective to shadows. The shadow cast by a river bank on the opposite side to where you are standing will be foreshortened. One of the more common mistakes is to forget that you are dealing in two different planes, just as with shadows that are cast on the ground. If, for example, you are looking down on some ducks in the reeds from a bridge, you will see the ducks and the reeds foreshortened from above, whereas you will see their shadows cast at right angles on the water face on.

▼ **Boys on the Lido** (oil on paper)
HAZEL SOAN
The strong evening light coming from behind the boys casts shadows and reflections that intertwine.

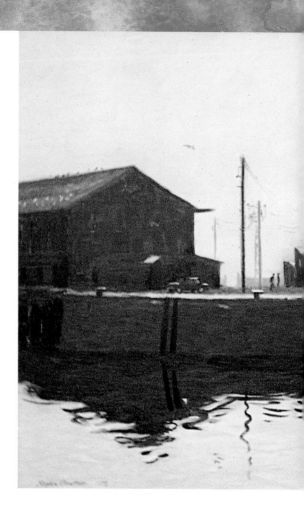

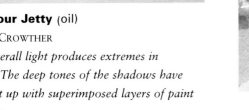

▲ **Harbour Jetty** (oil)

STEPHEN CROWTHER

Bright overall light produces extremes in contrast. The deep tones of the shadows have been built up with superimposed layers of paint and glazes.

Shadows and Reflections

Trees in the middle of the flooded Limpopo River, with the light behind them, cast reflections and shadows that extend toward the viewer.

1 *Map out the landscape with gentle watercolor washes wet-in-wet. Leave a light area in the middle of the river.*

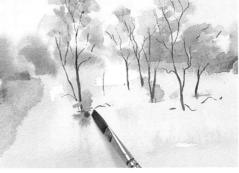

2 *Put in the trees: leaves first, branches next with a fine brush. Now wet the river with clean water where you want the reflections to go and feed in a darker brown.*

3 *Take the wash on down the page, feeding more color into the wet area as you go. Remember that the color will dry much paler and more blended than when wet.*

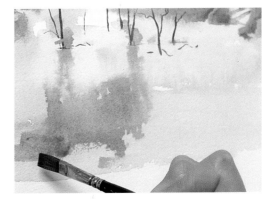

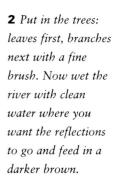

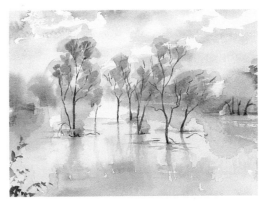

4 *Now add the tree shadows over the water, wet-on-dry, to give them sharper edges. The shadows should be the same color as the sky and extend from the bases of the trees.*

Light

As any artist knows, light is the most difficult thing of all to paint. Yet it is a feeling of light that brings a painting alive and it is a particularly important part of painting water. A lake will look very different according to the quality of the light, the time of day, and the season. Light creates reflections on the surface, causes ripples to sparkle and glint, and lets you look down into the depths of the water.

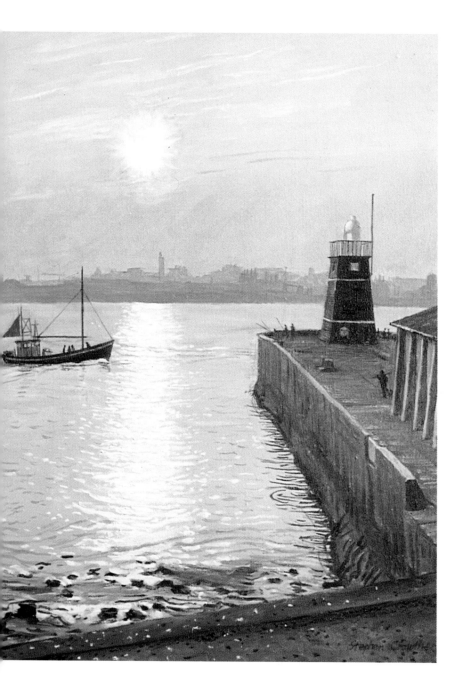

As with any painting, before you begin it is a good idea to work out the direction of the light and the position of the sun in the sky. On a sunny day this is easy, but on a cloudy day, light appears to come from the whole sky creating a diffused, overall effect – dull if the cloud is thick, and bright if it is thin. The direction of the light will affect the highlights on the water and shadows.

There is a subtle difference between reflections of the sky and reflections of direct light from the sun. The sun lights up the sky which can be reflected on the surface of the water. If the water is broken in any way, direct rays of light will then create bright highlights so that reflections of a blue sky can be fragmented by "white" ripples catching brighter light from the sun.

Strength and color

On water which is flat and clear like a mirror, the stronger the light, the brighter and more distinct the reflections. In poor light, the water appears dark and only bright tones will be reflected. If the water is ruffled, the pattern of reflected light will then depend

Return at Sunset (oil)
STEPHEN CROWTHER
When painting with oils, you can superimpose the bright pathway of the setting sun on the water at the end, in small impasto strokes that themselves reflect the light.

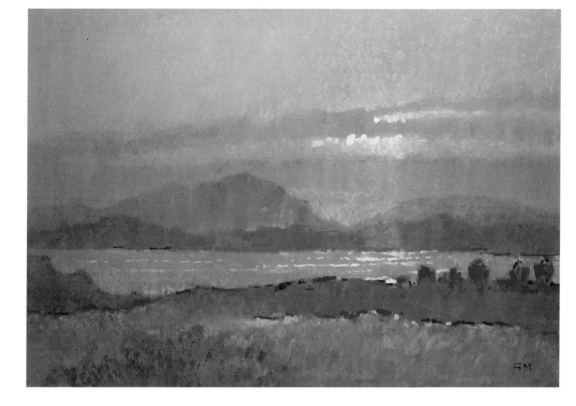

◀ **Sunset, Sea of Galilee** (pastel)
GEOFF MARSTERS
The warm tinted ground shows through the superimposed scumbles, but the exquisite luminosity comes from the bold touches of pale and golden yellow.

on where the sun is, whether the sun is behind you catching the sloping angles of each wavelet, or in front of you, highlighting the tops of each ripple.

The angle of the light makes a difference too, whether the sun is overhead as it is at midday or low as it is at sunrise or sunset. The season will make a difference as the sun never reaches great heights in the winter. With the sun high in the sky, the whole sky is bright and touches of direct reflected light are lost amongst the bright pattern of reflections. With the sun low in the sky, the colors are mellower and the tones deeper so that the reflections of the golden evening sun show up against the contrasting shadows.

Watercolor Wash on Grainy Paper

A simple way of painting a pathway of sparkling light across water is to use the texture of the paper. A little practice is needed to get the correct consistency of paint and sweep of the brush.

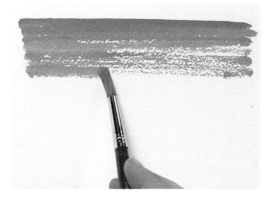

1 *Load a coarse, round brush with a not-too-dilute wash of blue and take it across the page in bold, horizontal strokes. Make your first attempts quite small. For a larger area, you will need a brush large enough to retain enough paint for a single stroke.*

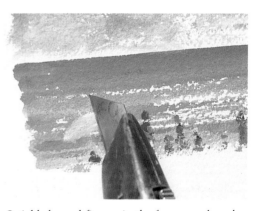

2 *Add sky and figures in the foreground, and the painting is nearly finished – just a few bands of darker blue are needed to vary the wash and hint at waves. If you want more touches of white in the water, you can use a craft knife to scrape off some of the blue paint.*

Wax Resist

Using a clear wax stick on rough paper, a broken path of white paper is reserved, and this repels the overlaid watercolor wash. When dry, the glimpses of white paper create a glittering path of light across the water.

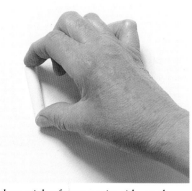

1 *Using a clear stick of wax on its side, make bold sweeps from one side of the paper to the other. Apply more pressure and the reserved white paper will be more solid.*

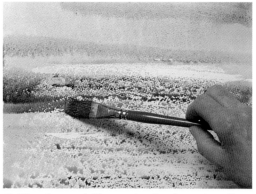

2 *Mix plenty of dilute paint for the main yellow wash and feed in other colors wet-in-wet for a striated wash. Remember that the color will dry paler.*

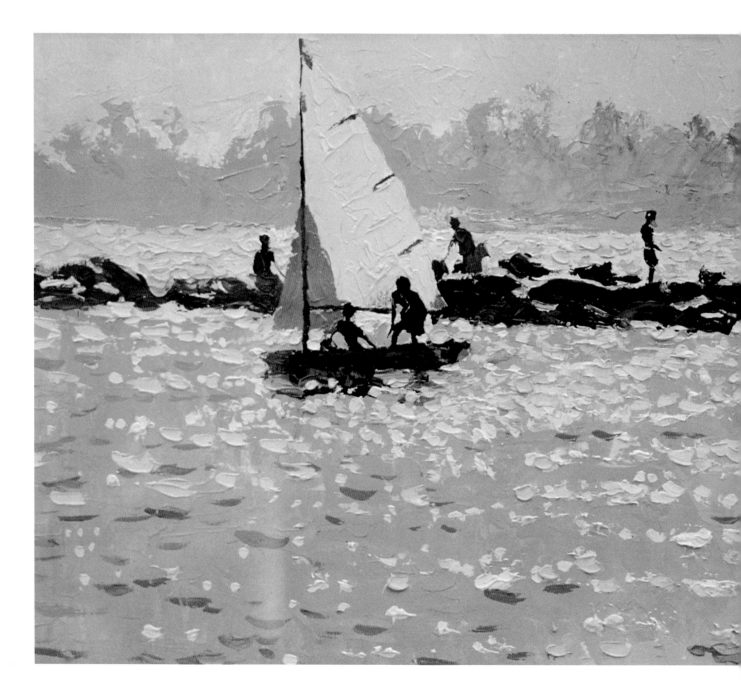

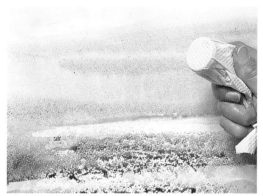

3 *Before the wash dries, wrap a suitable tube in paper towels (a film canister is used here) and press it firmly into the paint to lift out a circle of paint for the setting sun.*

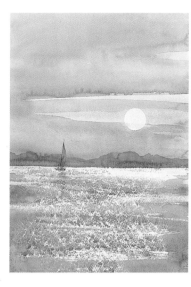

4 *Add more pink washes in the sky wet-on-dry, turning and bending the paper to form back runs. Add in a strip of land on the horizon and finally – using a pen loaded with watercolor – a lone yacht enjoying an evening sail.*

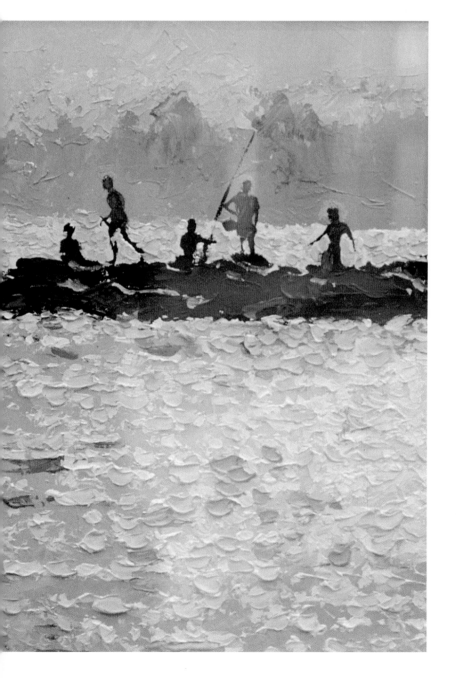

Light nearly always leans toward a color – we talk about golden evening light, a pink misty light or a cold blue light. With watercolors you can insure this light is carried through the painting by applying a wash of pale yellow, pink or blue at the start. With oils or acrylics, you can afford to be bolder with a strong mid-tone yellow ocher underpainting or warm pink. The same effect can be achieved with tinted papers for pastels. In each case the initial overall tinting will come through in small patches over the whole painting.

Highlights

It is worth remembering that points of light on the water surface can only be seen as such if they are contrasted with darks at the other end of the tonal scale – meaning that pure, brilliant white needs to be balanced with darkest black if it is to look white. Highlights are rarely purest white. They are usually broken with a little of the color of the predominant light – for example, pinkish in

◀ **Messing About in Boats** (oil)
HAZEL SOAN
The sparkling water seen in the evening light is added with touches of impasto, using a brush, over a flat layer of murky blues. Note how the light catches the edges of these impasto strokes.

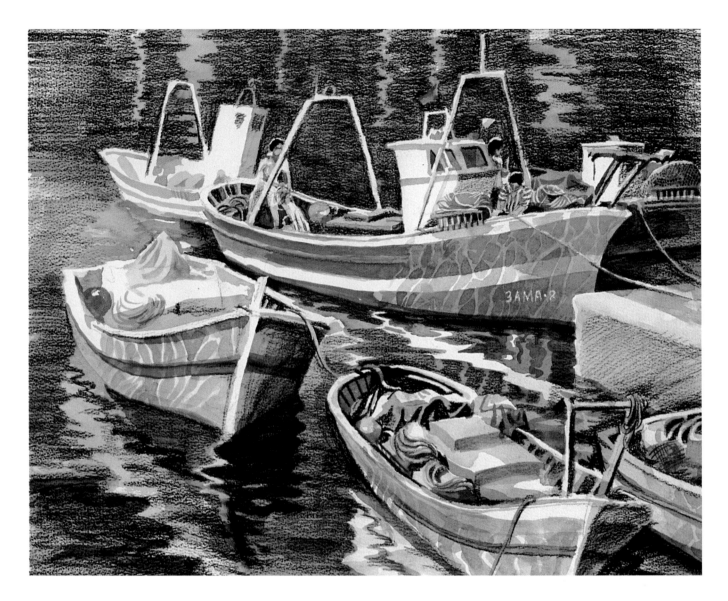

▲ **Fishing Fleet**
(conté over
watercolor)
HAZEL SOAN
*The pattern of light
reflected off the
water is clearly
visible on the sides
of the boats.*

the early morning and blue at midday, depending on the weather and season. Or pure white can be applied and partially blended into the color below. Working wet-in-wet with oils or acrylics, this breaking of the white is done by placing a loaded brush into wet color.

With watercolor, you will be surprised at how out of place pure white looks if you reserve highlights with liquid frisket. When you remove the fluid, these highlights often appear blindingly white and need to be knocked back with a quick wash of very pale color. With pastels, you can slightly blend white highlights with the color already applied by twisting the chalk as you make the mark.

Light is reflected back onto vertical surfaces, making patterns of light over a

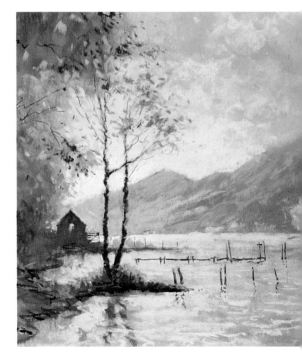

boat's painted hull, for instance. Such things are not always obvious, but if you know they are there, you can look for them, and hint at them in your painting to bring it to life. Such fragments of light can also be seen superimposed on reflections of the sky or surroundings. It is another way of projecting the illusion of water.

Composition and light

If you study a stretch of still water carefully, you will notice that it is echoing everything around it. However, as soon as the water is even slightly ruffled by a breath of wind, the tips of the ruffles catch the light and these fragments of light can appear across a whole stretch of water if the sky is very bright. However, if the light is coming from a single source, such as the sun or moon sitting low in the sky or lights along a river bank, it creates a sparkling, reflected path across the water. Touches of reflected light can be used to map out an area of water, leading the eye into the depths of the painting.

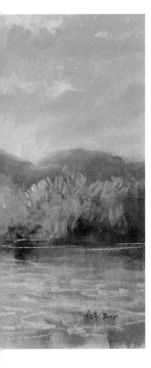

◄ **Derwent Water** (pastel)
ALAN OLIVER
For a pale, luminous evening light on the water, palest pink has been scumbled over darker, blended blues.

Reserving Lighter Areas with Liquid Frisket

When using water-based paints, you can reserve areas of white highlights with liquid frisket.

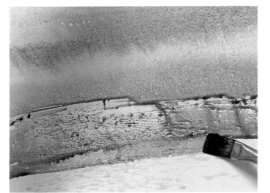

1 *Reserve a path of light by applying liquid frisket with the end of the brush handle. When the fluid is dry, gray wash over the area, feeding in color as you go.*

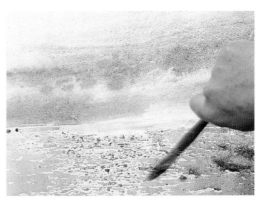

2 *Before the wash dries, flick on a few spots of a dilute dark color across the sky and in the water to add more tone. Take off some paint on the horizon with a clean rag.*

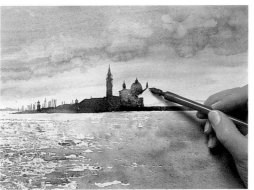

3 *Having built up the sky washes, add the distant Venetian skyline in a blue-black using a pen loaded with watercolor.*

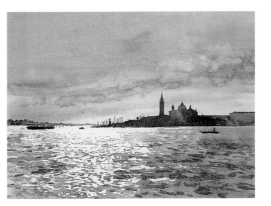

4 *Having checked that the paint is quite dry, rub off the liquid frisket with a clean finger. Add the final darker tones over the sea area wet-on-dry.*

Because these points of light can appear across the whole surface of a stretch of water, they can unify it. Reflected light can also help to bring the eye back to the surface of the water where there is a tendency to follow a reflection down into the depths. You can use reflected light for this purpose alone, putting in a touch here and there just to plot the surface of the water across the canvas.

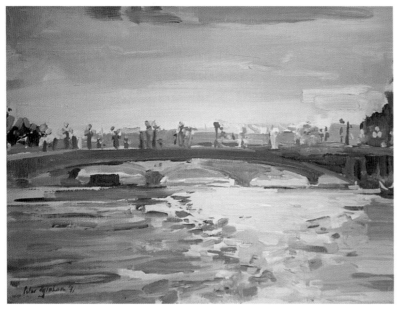

▲ **Pont Alexandre III** (oil)

PETER GRAHAM

A painting suffused with pink light, but note how dabs of pure color enliven the area of light reflected on the water.

Wet-in-Wet Oil Sketch Alla Prima

The ripples around this swimming child fragment the reflected colors of the surroundings – a complicated exercise in color and tone. When using oils, you can add and qualify colors and tones while the paint is wet.

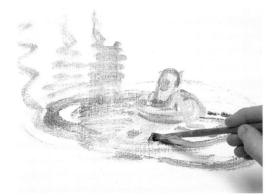

1 *Block in the main areas with mid-tone colors to get a feeling for the subject. Use bold strokes and avoid becoming bogged down in detail.*

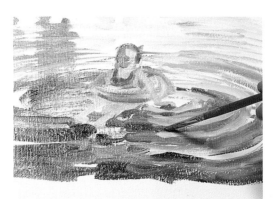

2 *Build up the darker, rippled sky tones reflected on the right, but keep applying separate strokes of color or you will lose the freshness of the exercise.*

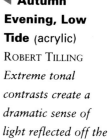

◀ **Autumn Evening, Low Tide** (acrylic)
ROBERT TILLING
Extreme tonal contrasts create a dramatic sense of light reflected off the surface of the water.

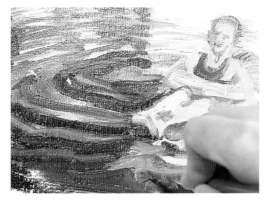

3 *Carefully observe and paint in the greens and browns on the left. And, to express the turbulence near the child's foot, try to make a juicy, twisted brushstroke.*

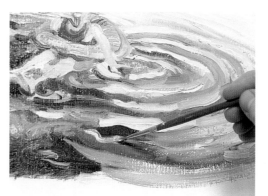

4 *Finally, add in the highlights, letting the wet paint already applied blend into the fresh brushstrokes to qualify the whiteness of the paint.*

Surface textures

Sometimes it is difficult to judge exactly where the surface of the water lies in a painting. Or you may finish a painting and find that the reflections and shadows in the water are confusing. This is particularly the case with still water. However, even if the evidence is not there, you can establish the water level with an indication of surface weed, or an opaque film of the sort seen on stagnant water, or some dirty foam along the edge of a canal.

To establish the surface plane of the water, you need not only to draw the eye to the surface but to unify the whole area – reflections of surroundings, the sky, shadows – so it can be read as water. You may need to improvise if the water you are painting is like a looking glass, suggesting the surface with a few strokes, as if the water is ruffled by a breeze. These can be hatched graphic strokes or a scumbled area over the reflection. To make this show up, you will have to apply light on dark, and dark on light.

Alternatively, you can paint in something floating or breaking through the surface of the water: reeds, or weed, surface scum whipped up by the wind, water fowl, or a mooring buoy on a lake.

Techniques to establish the surface plane

To establish the surface with watercolor, you can take off streaks of white with clean water with a cloth wrapped around your

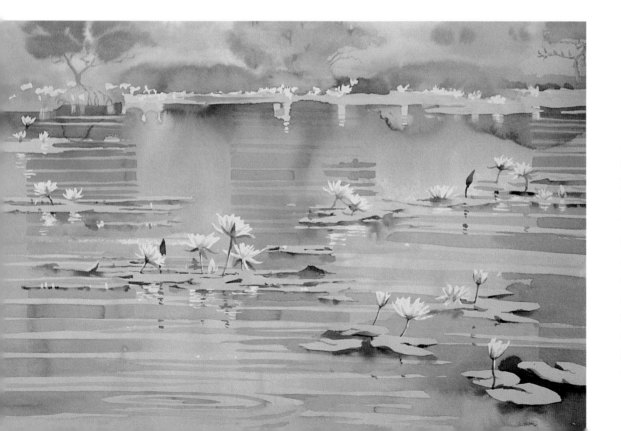

◀ **The River Waits, Okavango Delta** (watercolor) HAZEL SOAN
The surface plane of the water is established by breaking up the glassy reflection with horizontal strokes of dilute paint applied wet-on-dry.

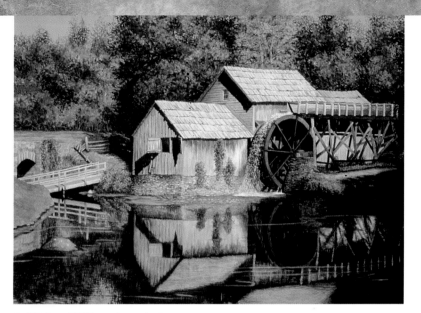

▲ **Mabry Mill** (watercolor)

RICHARD FRENCH

To unify the surface of the water, the artist trails subtle current lines across the reflections.

finger before the paint is too dry. Or, if you want to hatch a few clear strokes of white in an area of dark paint, wait until the paint is quite dry and then scrape through to the white paper beneath with a scalpel.

Sometimes with oils, or acrylics, where the paint retains the brushmark, the horizontal grooves left by the brush reflect the light and pull the eye back to the surface of the painting and the water. You can scumble or drybrush a gray "breeze" over dry paint, or scrape back through wet paint to the white canvas with the brush end.

With pastels, graphic strokes over a build-up of blended color will establish the surface plane. You can create a sharp edge to get a clean line with sandpaper or by cutting the stick with a scalpel or razor blade.

Lifting Off

To establish the surface plane of the water, the watercolor paint is lifted off with clean paper towels, revealing the white paper beneath.

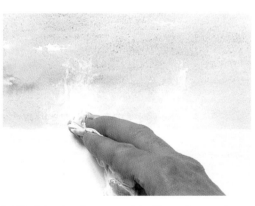

1 *Wash in the sky area with dilute ultramarine. Then take off the paint where the trees are to go using clean, scrunched-up paper towels, which will make them stand forward from the landscape.*

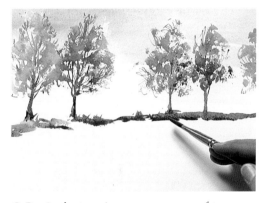

2 *Put in the trees in a narrow range of tones as the light is behind them.*

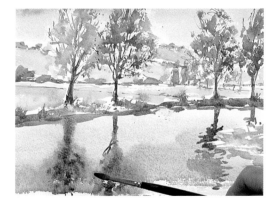

3 *Add the landscape around the trees and wash in the river, adding more color toward the near bank. Quickly add the reflections wet-in-wet.*

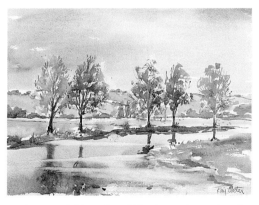

4 *Again quickly, take off horizontal streaks of paint with paper towels and establish the surface plane of the water.*

Urban waterscapes

We tend not to associate cities with waterscapes. Yet most major cities of the world are set on rivers and have canals, landscaped ponds, and fountains, as well as indoor pools. Another chance to paint the reflective qualities of water comes after a heavy downpour on tarmacked city streets and sidewalks.

City rivers offer the artist a host of subjects – river traffic, barges and ferries, as well as the machinery of the working port with cranes and davits. Reflections of waterside houses, rather than trees, can be a good place to start studying reflections as it is easier to see how they work and how they are affected by changes in the light and the state of the water. Water in such sheltered city rivers is often calmer, with hard weather only just upsetting the surface. Tidal rivers, such as the Thames in London, provide ideal water

Building up White Water

Using acrylics thickly, you can build up from dark to light by starting with the shadows and adding the highlights last. The soft edges of this row of fountains give the impression of water shooting up and splashing down again.

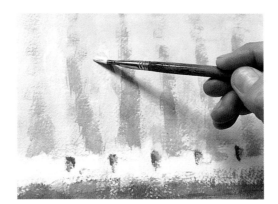

1 *Over an ocher background, plot out the darker and mid-tone shadows in the fountain's columns of water.*

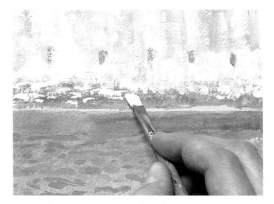

2 *Build up the whiter highlights on the fountains in broken strokes of white, and then stipple in the water splashing below.*

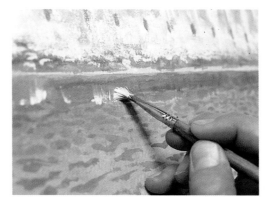

3 *Paint on the splashes of water with a dry brush. First clean a hogshair brush with a cloth, and then take up a little undiluted white. Touch it onto the surface and brush it upward.*

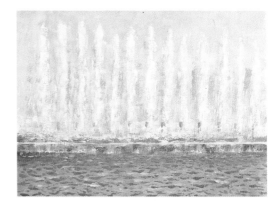

4 *Build up layers of broken paint that let the color beneath show through, which will create soft-edged columns of frothing water that are not too solid and appear to be moving.*

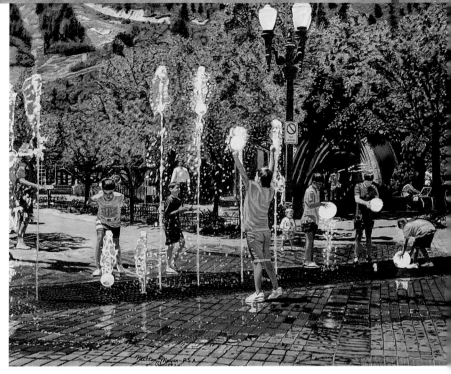

subjects. At low tide mud-covered banks stay wet, reflecting the sky above.

A particularly romantic urban river view can be seen in the early evening or at night. A city generates its own light, letting you make out the shapes of buildings against the night sky. Also, city rivers are often plotted with street lights along the banks, pinpoints of light reflecting across the river in an almost monochrome tonal landscape. Combined with the light of a dying sunset, the effect can be impressive, although you have to be careful not to let your painting become over-sentimental. Even though nature is sometimes too good to be true, glorious technicolor sunsets reflected in the water look false when reproduced faithfully.

Fountains

Fountains these days come in every shape (and color when lit up at night). In the city, they are designed to complement the architecture, to act as a form of punctuation in the cityscape. Painting fountains of water is more difficult than it might seem. Often the shooting column of water, which is mainly "white" water, looks too solid. Being white water, it does behave like a solid white column, with the light falling on it on one side, casting a shadow on the other. You can be too literal, however, and, rather like painting surf or waterfalls, the artist has, above all, to capture both the texture and the movement of the water.

Like so many other aspects of painting water, it is a good idea to study the "structure" of the spouting water in a photograph as it is difficult to see what is going on when it is moving so fast. Don't copy it slavishly, though, or it will look static; blur the outline and create a sense of movement with textural techniques such as scumbling and spattering.

Wet streets

Rainwater remains on the surface of unabsorbent materials making slate roofs, sidewalks and tarmac roads glisten in the brighter light after the clouds have passed. A wet street reflects light from the sky and street lights and, when it is truly wet, it will reflect other elements in the picture, such as people and street furniture.

▲ **Summer Fun in Aspen, Colorado** (pastel)
MILTON MEYER
White, gray and blue are worked over the background for the water spouts. Note the intensification of color on the wet paving.

▶ **Taxi in the Kings Road** (watercolor)
HAZEL SOAN
Liquid frisket is used to isolate the splashes, and the reflections are simplified into three basic, superimposed tones.

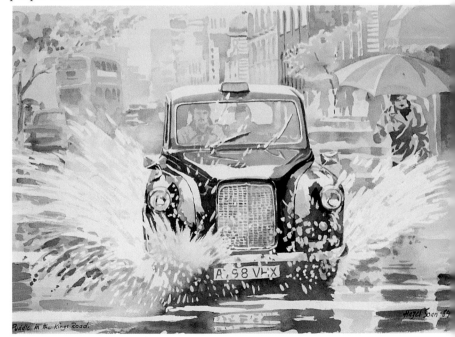

Lights on an Urban River

An urban river in the Far East is painted in the pale yellow evening light. The colors and tones are kept subdued with the final points of light added to the pagoda and then brought down and touched on the water.

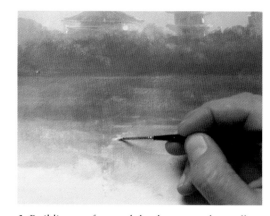

1 *Building up from subdued tones, palest yellow is scumbled over the water to establish the horizontal plane. Then bright points of white tinted with cadmium yellow light up the pagodas.*

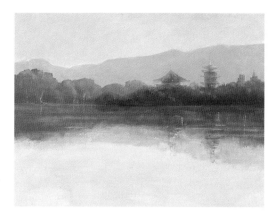

2 *In the finished painting you can see how the artist has checked any dramatic gestures in color and tone so that those final touches of light capture the glint of sun on gold.*

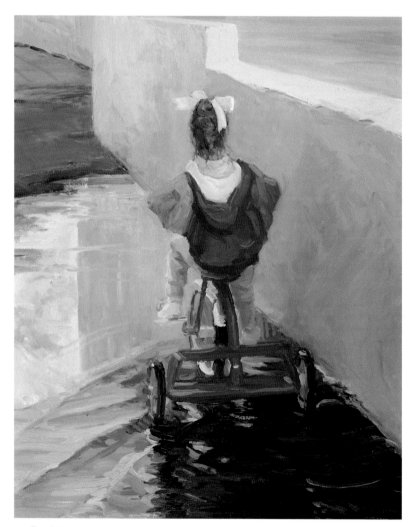

▲ **Puddle Jumper** (oil)

DENISE BURNS

In the small area of water the artist deals with reflections and shadows, broken water and movement, and establishes the integration of puddle and concrete.

Reflections in wet streets and puddles are often dominated by verticals snaking their way toward you. You need only look at the examples on this page. These snake-like strokes tell you that what you are looking at is a reflection in water, rather than a shadow on dry land. With opaque media, you can run the brush through the built-up paint for these wiggling reflections, or use the brush-end sgraffito-style to create lighter reflections. For watercolor you will have to reserve pale reflections at the outset but darker ones can be added at the end. A painter may ask himself if the result does indeed look wet. Reflections on the streets and heightened contrasts will help to put across the wetness of the scene, as will scurrying rain clouds and people carrying umbrellas.

Puddles can make a subject in themselves as can be seen on this page, or they can be used to great effect in a composition, creating patches of reflected light along a dark road. For the city dweller, a puddle is a convenient way to study water and how it behaves in relation to light.

Swimming pools

As a category of water, swimming pools are hard to place. With wave machines and water jets, not to mention motion caused by swimming and diving, still water becomes

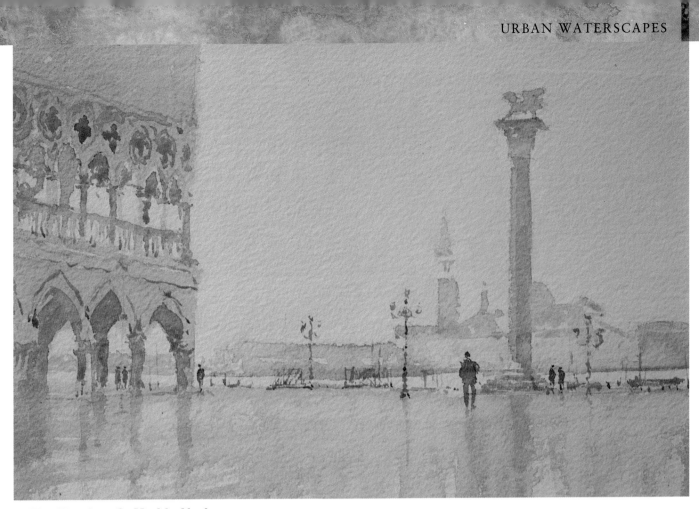

▲ **Wet Morning, St Mark's, Venice**

(watercolor)

ALAN OLIVER

A simple, almost monochrome painting in which delicate washes represent the reflections caused by a diffused, pale yellow light.

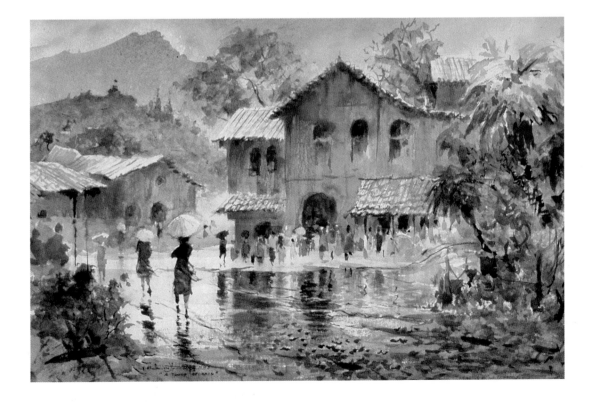

◀ **A Touch of Rain** (watercolor)

LAVERE HUTCHINGS

Heavy rainfall floods the street and turns it into a patchwork of reflected color, captured with washes, wet-in-wet and then wet-on-dry.

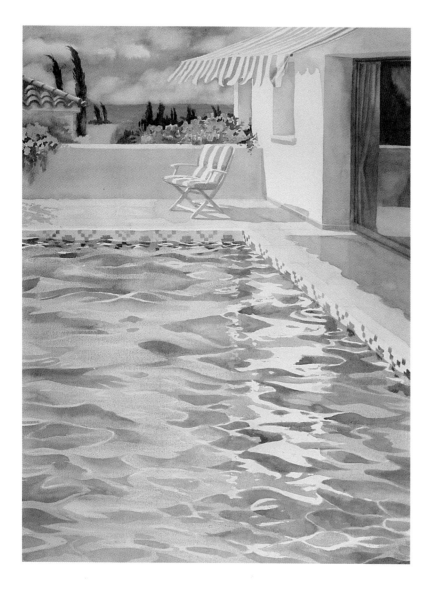

◀ **Small Breeze from the Sea** (watercolor)
HAZEL SOAN
The broken water is built up in superimposed washes with harder edges in the foreground.

moving water. Whatever the definition, pools are an attractive subject to paint either indoors or outdoors. A swimming pool is a useful subject for learning how water reflects and catches the light and of studying what forms look like underwater, without getting too involved with the problems of distance.

The standard pool, painted in shades of blue and green and reminiscent of tropical waters, is associated in our minds with leisure time. If you look back at vacation photographs, you can see how light from the sun not only reflects off the surface of the water where it is disturbed, but also is refracted onto the sides and bottom of the pool, so that you have two levels of light patterns. If you look at the paintings of David Hockney, the British painter who has lived and worked amongst the swimming

pools of San Francisco for many years, you see how he reduces these reflections to a repetitive pattern to suit his need for a background for his figurative studies.

Swimming pools are a good place to study the appearance of bodies under water. We know that the water itself is not blue but the blue of the sides of the pool is reflected onto the body under water so it will take on a bluish tinge. If the pool were red, the body under water would take on a reddish tinge. The deeper the body, the less light reaches it and so the bluer it appears, and the less sharp will be the focus.

The water also acts like a lens, distorting the form of the body, making it generally larger. As with glass, if the water is swirling about the "lens" distorts and the view of the body is distorted too. Add to this patches of reflections and light on the broken surface and the outline of the form under water is further distorted. Finally, refracted light will striate the body with golden stripes. Sunlight will reflect directly off the body above the water and very close to the surface, but not far below.

Photographs are very useful tools when studying these aspects of pool life. They freeze the moment, making it simple to see what exactly is going on. You can then add the sensation of movement in your interpretation of that photograph. And next time you are painting a similar scene, you can incorporate the wisdom acquired in your previous observations. Remember, too, that these observations are relevant to any body or object in any water – swimming pools are just a useful means of studying them.

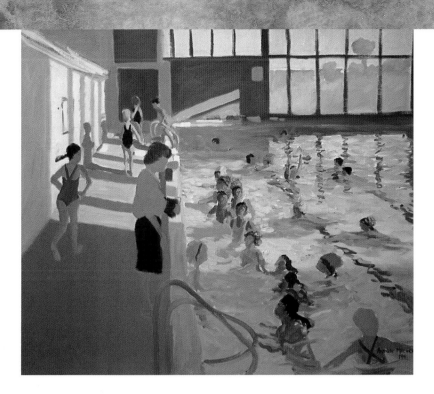

◀ **Pool, Moorways, Derby** (oil)

ANDREW MACARA

A display of various options within a pool: sky reflections, and water in light and in shadow. Small superimposed strokes made wet-in-wet capture the constant changes of color.

Superimposing Thin Glazes

Oil paint can be built up in thin glazes of transparent paint to create a rich translucency. The first layer can be diluted with turpentine and the last layers with glazing medium, which makes colors more transparent.

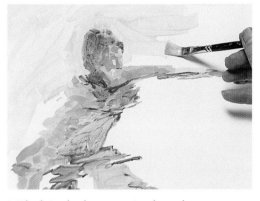

1 *Block in the figure, noting how the water distorts the outline. Then add a thin glaze of transparent cerulean blue mixed with a little monestial turquoise thinned with turpentine.*

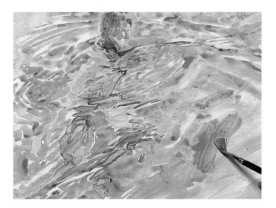

2 *When the first layer is dry, brush on another, less dilute layer of the same color, mixed with glazing medium, in uneven strokes, cutting around the highlights.*

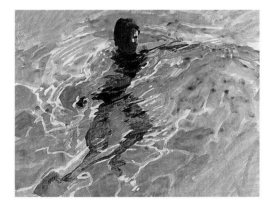

3 *Add another layer of blue to intensify the color and tone around the swimmer. Finally, balance the highlights with dilute white knocked back with a touch of the shadow color.*

Pulling it together

When painting water, you must consider integrating it into the picture as a whole. Sometimes, if you treat it too separately, water refuses to merge into the landscape. The problem arises because water *is* different, and the artist has to show this while pulling it into the painting through technical harmony, color, and compositional lines.

You can pull a painting together by maintaining a consistent approach across the whole picture surface. One way of doing this is by using a repetitive brushstroke which gives a cohesive appearance to the painting – a short vertical stroke, for example, or small dots as the pointillistes did. With water, however, the flat horizontal plane begs for different treatment and many artists will paint water with consistent horizontal strokes and the surrounding landscape with a multitude of different techniques. In such a case, other ways of pulling the painting together will have to be investigated.

Color and composition

Color will do the job for you. By consciously taking certain colors across the picture surface – from the water, to the surroundings, up to the sky – this will help to unify the disparate elements of the painting. Reflections

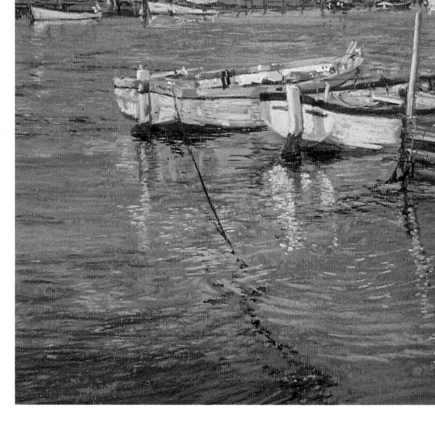

▶ **Afternoon Sun, Walberswick** (pastel)
MARGARET GLASS
Boats, ropes and a jetty create complicated reflections, and these are unified by the golden-brown tinted paper showing through the broken pastel strokes.

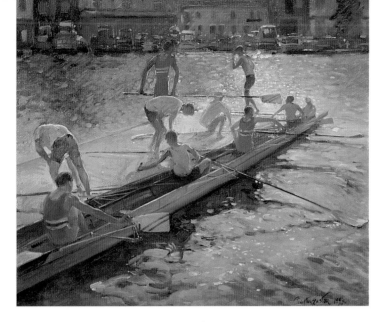

▶ **At the Jetty, Henley** (oil)

TIMOTHY EASTON

A limited palette is used and colors are taken across the painting, giving it a sense of unity. For example, the eye picks up on the lilac vest of the oarsman and travels to his oar, to highlights in the water and then to the boats in the background.

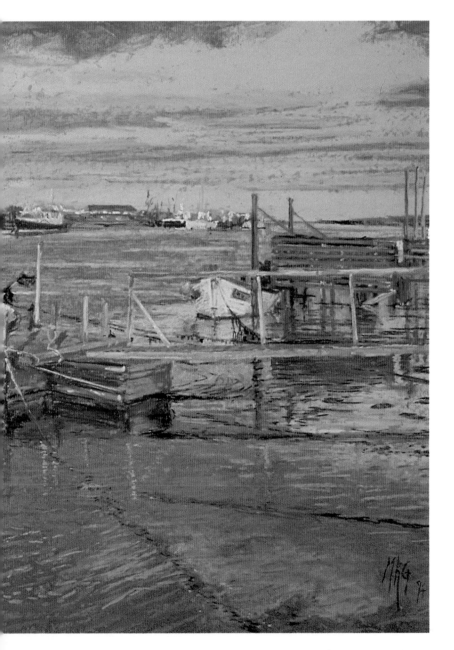

of the surrounding landscape in the water help in this respect, by taking the eye from one to the other. Similarly, using a tinted ground will also help to pull the painting together if you let small patches show through the paint overall. Tinted paper of a range of colors and tones is sold for use with pastels.

If you find the different parts of your composition too separate, you can unite them, or put them in the same plane, by linking them visually. A woodland pond may seem isolated from its surrounding landscape so you can link it by an overhanging branch which crosses from the surroundings to the water, or with yellow flag irises which take the eye from the water to the landscape. Vertical mooring posts on a lake will have the same effect, linking sky with water.

Whitewater textures

An area of water can fall out of synchronization with the rest of the painting if you treat it in isolation. It is so easy to get carried away with a certain area of the painting, particularly where water is concerned, and overwork that area, bringing it on far beyond the rest of the painting.

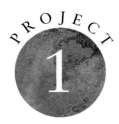
Strong Contrasts

A swimming pool on a bright, sunny day. But there is not much heat in the sun and the artist puts this across by emphasizing cooler colors, particularly in the shadows. The artist works on the surroundings to the pool first, leaving the water until last. The shadows and reflections on the surface of the water and on the sides and bottom of the pool are built up with translucent washes.

Materials used

**140 watercolor paper
(16 × 12 inches)**
●
Watercolor paints: cerulean blue, cobalt green, rose madder, Indian yellow, yellow ocher, burnt umber, French ultramarine.
●
Brushes: ½-inch flat, large soft round sable watercolor sizes 0, 2 and 12.
●
Pencils
●
Eraser
●
Metal ruler
●
Kitchen paper
●
Nibbed pen

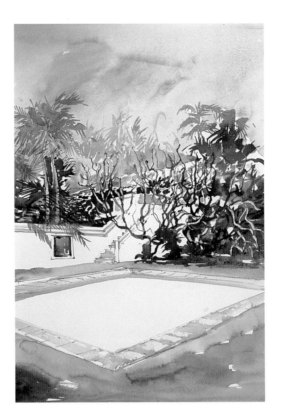

1 *Start with a simple sketch and then paint in the surroundings to the pool. Even though the view is limited, be conscious of the effects of aerial perspective on the background, making the trees paler and bluer and less distinct. Conversely, those closer to are shown in stark contrast against the white wall, their shadows creating an interesting pattern.*

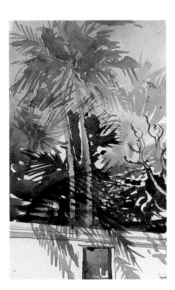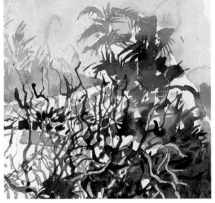

2 *Paint the trees (left) over the sky wash when it is dry, making the mix paler for the distance. Map out the branches against the wall (above) with a nibbed pen loaded from a brush.*

3 *Lay down the pool surround with a pale yellow wash. When dry, add shadows with Indian yellow broken with a neutral mix. Strengthen the outlines with pen.*

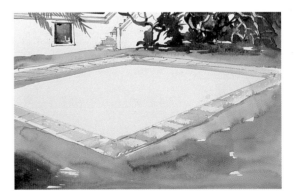

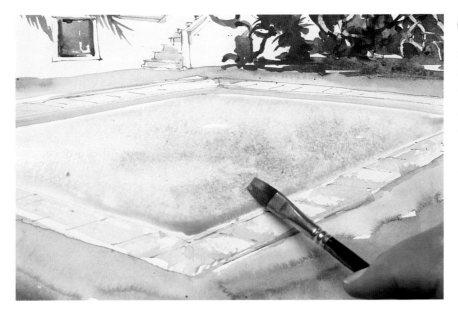

4 Wash in the pool with a mix of cerulean blue and cobalt green, with a little more green for the shadows stippled in wet-in-wet. Bend the paper to move the paint where you want it.

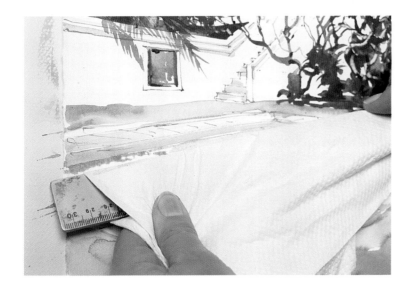

5 Quickly, before the paint dries, wrap some paper towels around a metal ruler and lift off the paint with a steady downward sweep to create the sunlit side of the pool.

6 Now add the reflection of the window in the wall on the pool using the square shape of the brush. Start off with pale washes if you are not sure. Watercolor dries paler, but you can always make it darker by superimposing another wash.

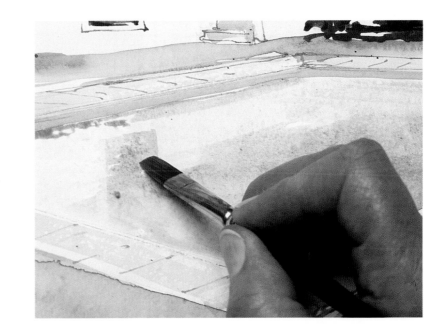

7 Shadows cast on the sides and bottom of the pool are added in a darker wash of the same color with a touch of cold French ultramarine added. These are painted wet-on-dry so that the edges are starker to capture the dappled reflections.

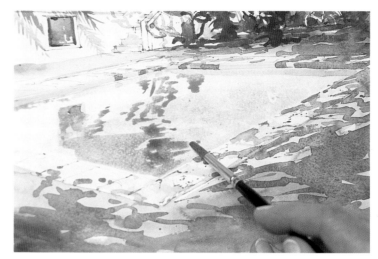

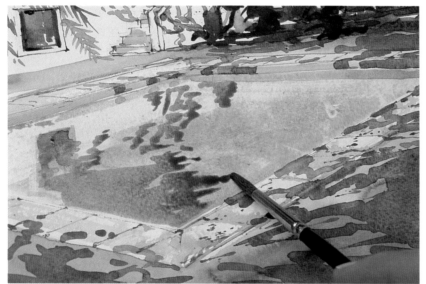

8 Build the tones up gradually, superimposing washes, or if you know they need to be darker, just touch the tip of your brush onto the wet surface to feed in darker tone.

9 When the paint is dry, darker touches are added with a smaller brush for the reflections on the surface of the pool, so that you have the impression that you are looking down through a number of levels of reflected light and shadow.

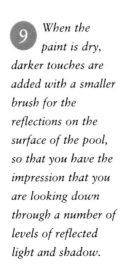

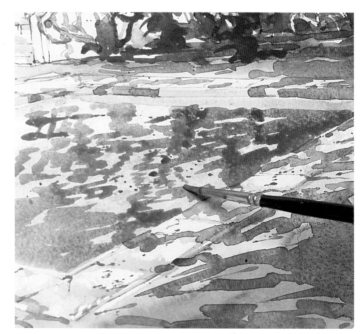

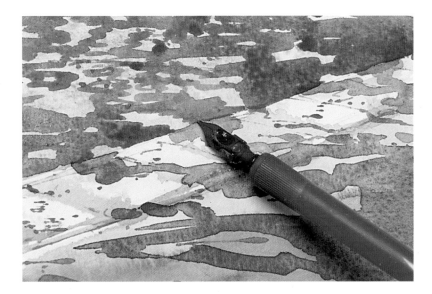

10 *Again, use the nibbed pen, loaded by your brush with watercolor, to trace linear marks over the surface of the pool. These lines are important to reinforce the surface plane of the water.*

▶ **Too Cold to Swim**

KAY OHSTEN

To balance the contrasts in the pool with those of the surroundings, the artist has added more layers of dilute paint. Note the carefully conserved edge of light gray along the water's edge of the far side – clarifying this dark corner.

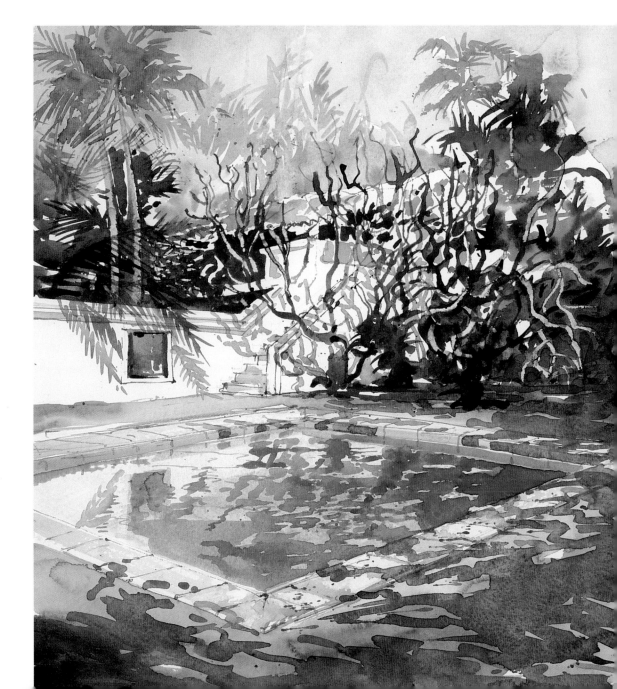

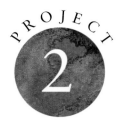

PROJECT 2

A Misty River

The weak, cold, misty light of a frosty morning is reflected off the flat surface of this slow-moving river. Starting with warm, sepia-tinted finest-grade sandpaper, the artist maps out the darker tones and then builds up the colors – more generalized at first and then with graphic linear work over the top. Note how the artist works from the background forward. The rough surface of the sandpaper means that you can build up the pastels like oil paint, letting you self-blend one color into another without rubbing.

Materials used

Chalk pastels: dark and light cool gray and warm gray, dark cerulean blue, pale and dark French ultramarine blue, mid-cobalt blue, sap green, burnt sienna, cadmium red, lemon yellow, cadmium yellow, pale cadmium orange. (These are general suggestions for this palette as color names and tint terminology vary between brands.)

●

Finest grade sandpaper

●

Brush

3 *The sky has been blended in with warm blue in the corners and cooler blue behind the trees, and a warm patch of yellow in the center for an illusion of aerial perspective. The cooler background color to the trees is added with loose strokes.*

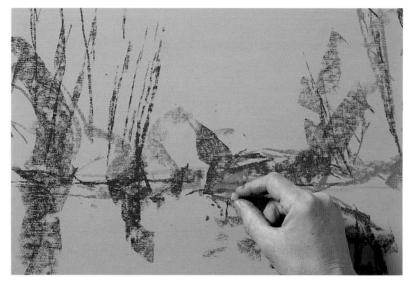

1 *Map out the composition working from dark to light. Make broad sweeps of a dark gray pastel stick held on its side, with linear strokes for trees.*

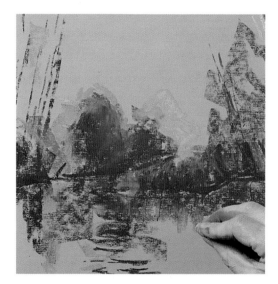

2 *Build up the darker tones with the dark gray. Keep on exploring the scene with mid-tone colors, working in sap green and burnt sienna with touches of cadmium red.*

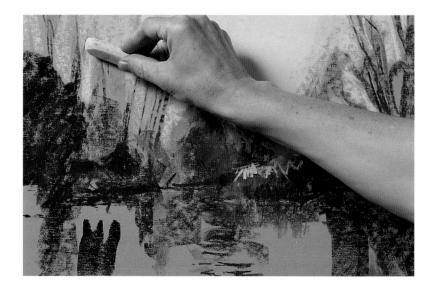

4 *Working on the background trees, a pale blue-gray is scumbled loosely over the top of the darker blue, softening the edges and pushing the trees back. Work with loose strokes on the mid-tone gray reflections.*

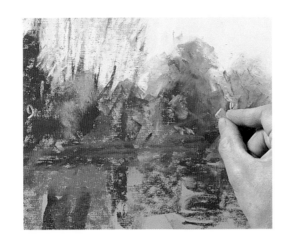

5 *Now build up the closer trees on the right where the colors and contrasts need to be sharper. With a sharp-edged chalk, make small jabbing strokes, twisting the chalk as you lift it off to make clear bright points of light. The underpainting is loose so these points will be sharper where the paper is untouched and therefore rougher.*

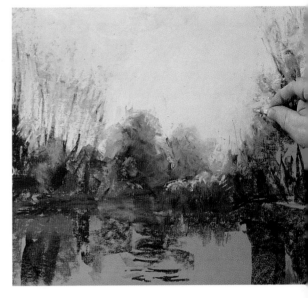

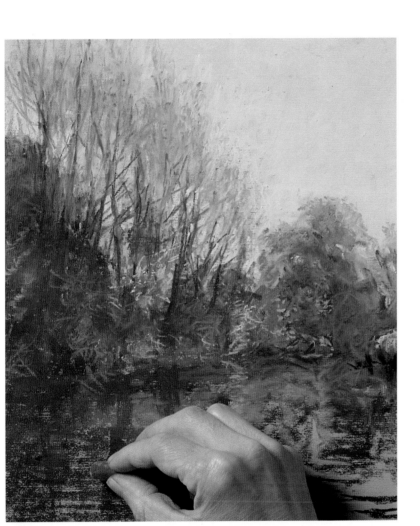

6 *For the shadowy area of the water, create streaks of light with loose horizontal lines over the early darks, letting the sepia of the paper show through. Build up the trees above with linear strokes, finishing with a frenzy of delicately placed colored strokes to enliven the area. Add points of color – yellow and red – to lift the tempo of the area.*

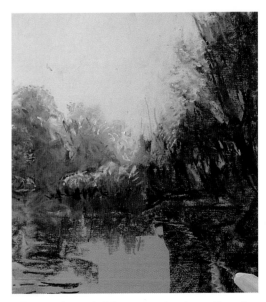

7 *With a pale blue, trace the zigzag line of the frosty water's edge. The line will bite more where the paper is uncovered with pastel, making it vary in tone.*

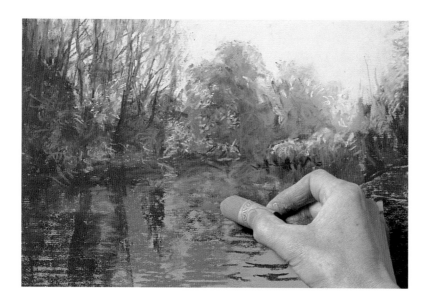

8 Return to the water and build up the mid-tone grays with more horizontal lines. At this stage these colors and tones of the reflections in the water are still separate. Unifying the area comes later.

9 The right-hand bank and its trees needs working on to balance it with, and bring it forward from, the left bank. Add more color to the trees – touches of yellow and burnt sienna. Then work on the bank, building up the darks with browns and grays.

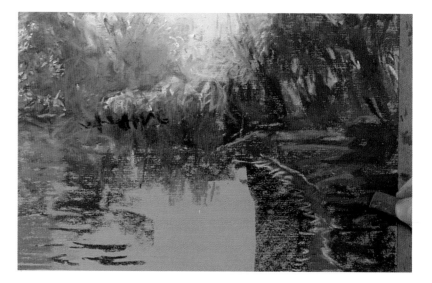

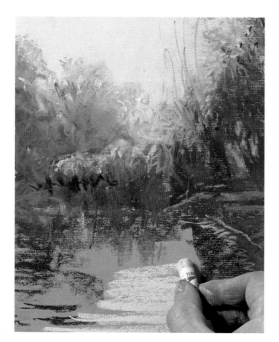

10 With a pale umber, add the patch of reflected sky in the water with strong horizontal strokes. Don't use either pure white as the light is not strong and reflections are never as bright or yellow as reflected color is usually duller.

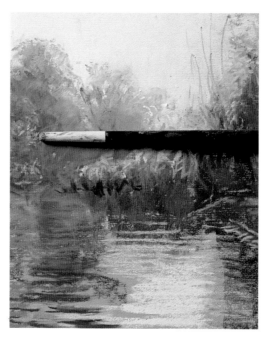

11 The area around the bright patch of reflected sky is worked on with pale blue horizontal strokes. Now is a good time to check that your reflections correspond to the landscape. Use a brushend or pencil to measure them as your eye can play tricks with you.

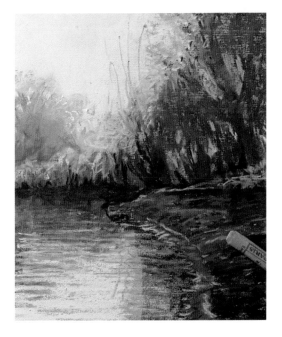

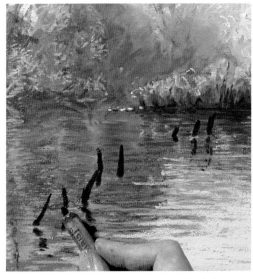

12 *Build up the horizontal lines of the reflections – picking out the yellow of the reeds, and the dark cerulean blue of the background trees. Then crisp up the bank with touches of a stronger ultramarine blue.*

13 *Add points of pink-white to lead the eye around, such as those on the far bend of the river. Finally, add corresponding darks in the line of irregular posts making the strokes strong and dark.*

▼ Cold Misty Morning

MARGARET GLASS

The posts force the eye to linger as it travels over the foreground and yet encourage it to explore the background.

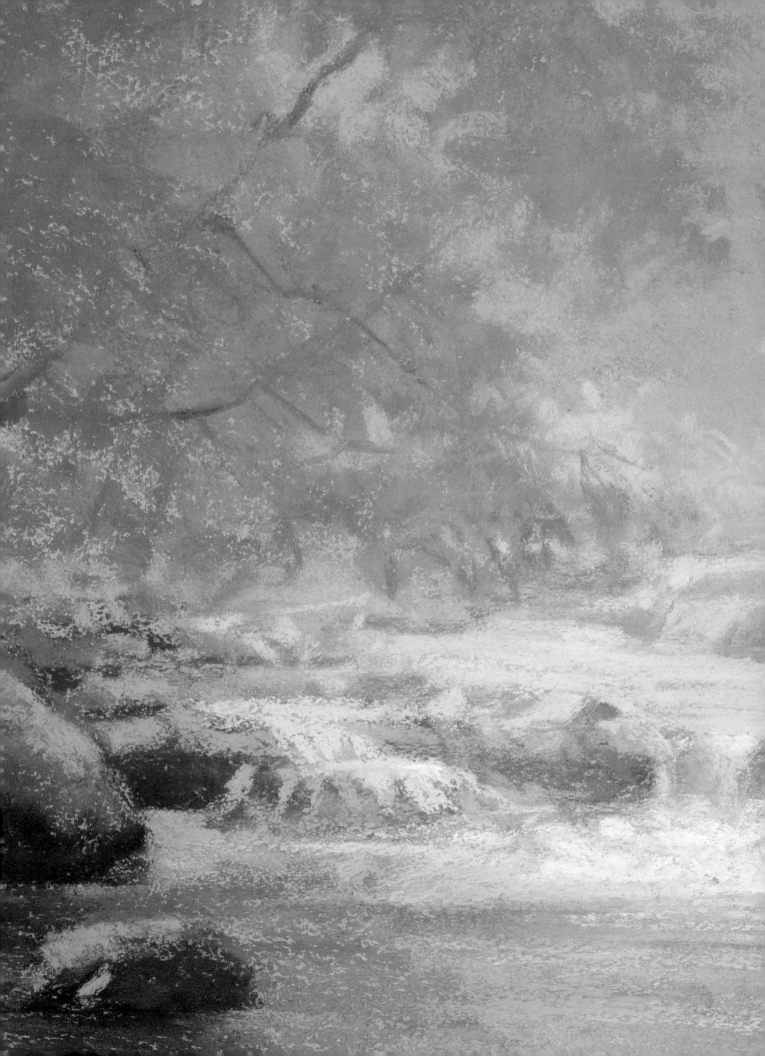

CHAPTER THREE

Moving water

Moving water can hypnotize with its surging, rhythmic power, and a river ½ mile wide will sweep along impressively. In a more dramatic fashion, huge waves crashing onto rocks, or water running fast in a mountain stream, are thrilling to watch. It is this evidence of a hidden force, found in all kinds of moving water, that the artist has to try to capture. The spray in the air, the power of the water, and its deafening sound – these are the invigorating feelings that have to come across in the painting, and that the artist needs to suggest.

Fall on the Flatland (pastel)
DOUG DAWSON
Water rushes over rocks into a deep pool, broad pastel strokes.

River water

Moving water in rivers is a vast topic. There are bubbling streams coursing over pebbles, and major rivers, murky with silt, which flow along with steady intent to the sea. You will find rivers in rain forests and the Grand Canyon; rivers such as the Limpopo, "all set about with fever trees;" and rivers that forge their way through the great capital cities of the world.

Extremes in the physical nature of rivers and streams, and in their location, are not the only factors affecting their appearance. All river water varies both in more obvious ways – in power and "color" – and in subtle ways. As the water trickles or surges along, you will see the surface change in character according to the obstacles it meets: gliding over pebbles, rippling off the bank, crashing down levels over rocks and debris, or turning back on itself in gentle eddies on the outside of a bend. In your paintings, you will be contriving to combine these different qualities using a variety of techniques.

As a painter of rivers, too, you will need to come to terms with river traffic – boats, barges and ferries – and with river wildlife, which is very much a part of the overall scene – fish, insects, birds, and rodents, as well as waterside trees and flowers.

▶ **Wintry Day** (oil)
MARTHA SAUDEK
Deep blues and golds are reflected in the icy stream, still running on a cold, sunlit day.

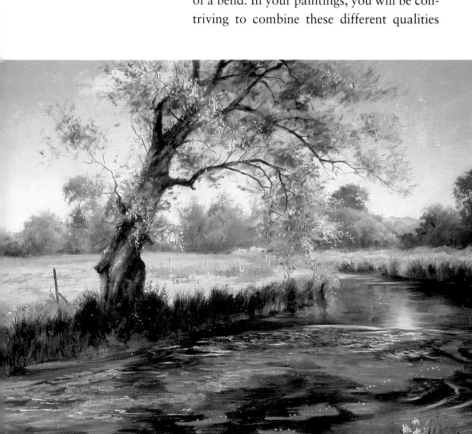

◀ **The Upper Test, Northington from near Overton** (oil)
WILLIAM GARFIT
The artist captures the changing state of the water as it sweeps round the bend and glides down the straight, disturbed where it runs over stones. There are reflections, patches of weed, areas of light and shade, and glimpses of the stony bed.

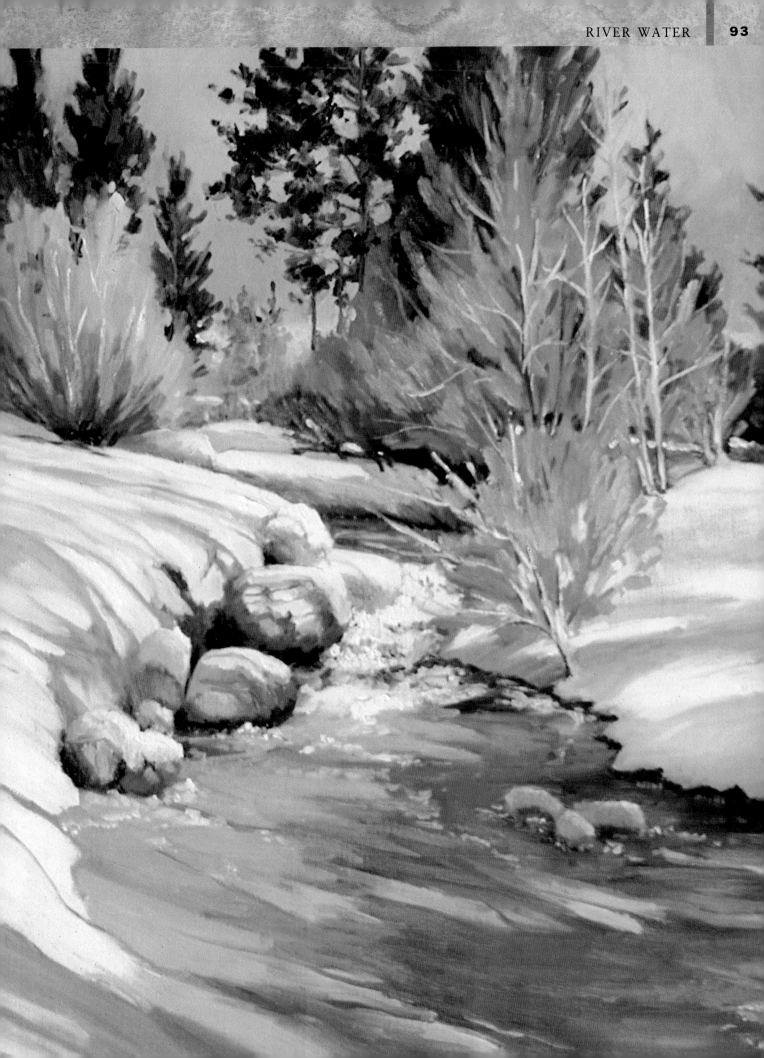

Photo ideas

Water is fascinating to watch and paint. You can paint the river flowing past you or focus in on one small part of it, such as a patch of boiling water where it passes over a patch of weed or protruding rock. These photographs of moving rivers may give you some ideas.

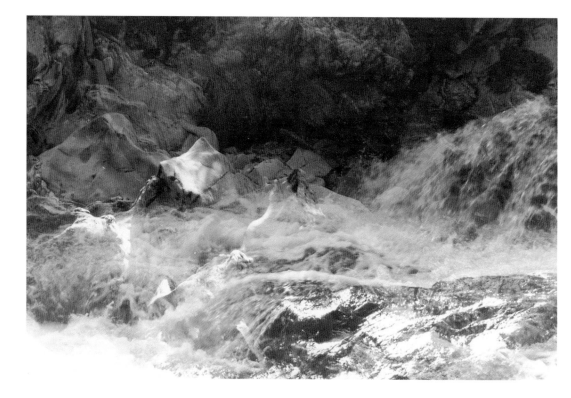

◄ **The Trossachs, Scotland**
Focusing right in on this rushing water makes a picture with abstract possibilities. With opaque paints, work mostly in subtle mid-tones leaving yourself the dimension of some dazzling pinky-whites for the highlights.

Water on Rocks ▶
If you adjust the exposure on your camera, moving water appears blurred, giving you some ideas on how to capture such water as it falls and splashes and bubbles its way between the rocks.

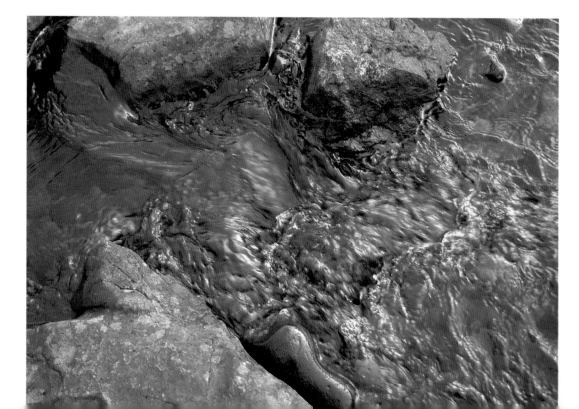

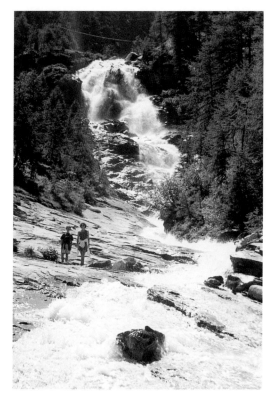

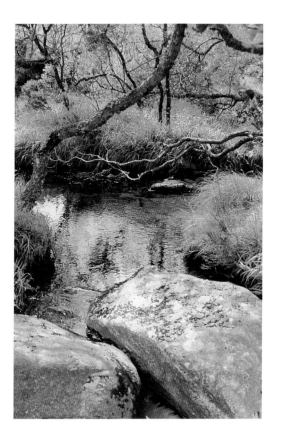

▶ Shady River, Devon

A quieter backwater of this river but there is still movement which breaks up the reflections. There is a nice passage worth developing where the stones are visible on the river bed through the shadow.

▲ Source of the Isère, France

The problem here is to paint the water in the background with less focus and detail than the foreground as it is not clear in the photograph. See how it is done in watercolor on page 100.

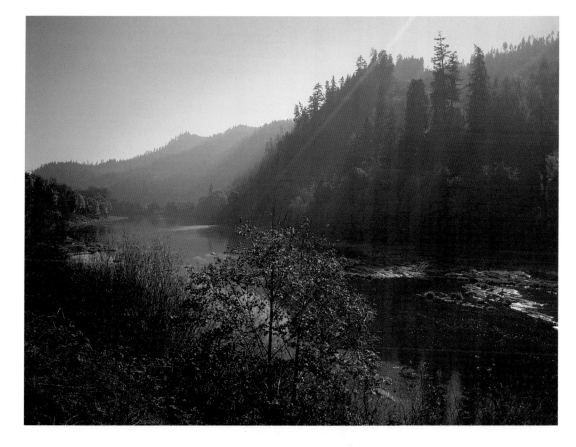

▶ Umpquar River, Oregon, USA

Seen from a distance, this fast-flowing river might appear still were it not for the patches of white water. The scene needs to be pulled together through linking colors: you can pick up on the yellows.

Making the water flow

Rivers, streams and bubbling brooks form a network across the land mass, like arteries and veins through a body, and are destined by gravity to flow from high ground down to the sea. One of the main problems faced by the painter of rivers is to capture this sense of movement – the water flowing along.

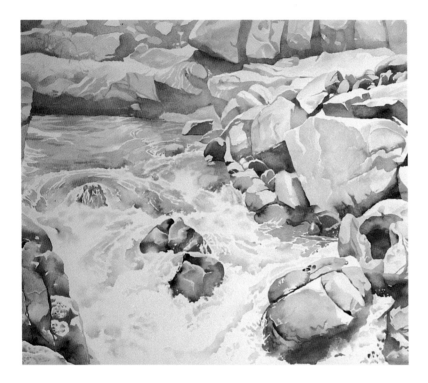

This movement in a river can be emphasized through careful planning of the composition. Place yourself where you can see a good stretch of the river, close enough and with a high enough viewpoint to enable you to see any movement on the surface. Include some clues to the speed of the water, such as rocks and stones breaking the surface of the water and causing it to boil around them. Wildlife elements that show the power of the current are useful indicators – willow fronds trailing

◀ **Cascade (Augrabies Falls)** (watercolor)
HAZEL SOAN
Note how the texture of the water is described as much by the edges of washes between areas of light and shade as by the physical application of paint.

Sgraffito and Other Techniques for Making Water Flow

The artist needs to hint at movement in the water even if it is not actually visible. With opaque paints, here acrylics, directional current lines can be scraped into the paint.

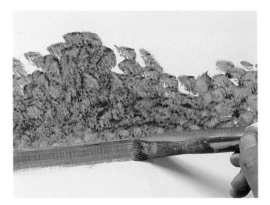

1 *First block in the foliage on the river bank with animated brushwork, creating patches of light and shade by varying the thickness of the paint. Then add in the river with steady, horizontal strokes, using a coarse bristle brush.*

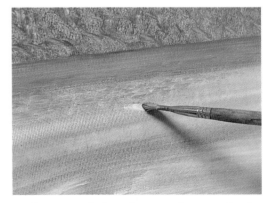

2 *The river is darker where it is deeper, under the bank. Paint in the rest of the water with a more dilute mix, with strokes that suggest the direction of flow. Add small, stippled strokes of the darker color for the stones on the river bed.*

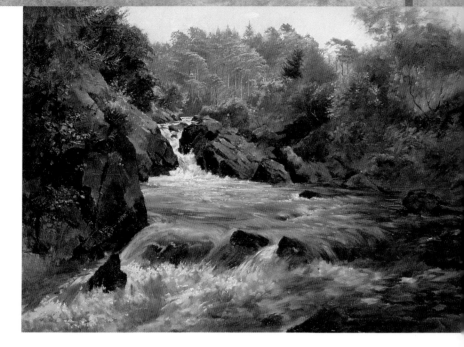

in the water or ripples bouncing off a semi-submerged tree trunk. River traffic, too, indicates the speed of the water – boats pulling against their moorings or a duck paddling hard against the flow.

Trails of underwater weed, if you can find them, are a good way to indicate the course of the current. They act rather like "whizz" lines in a cartoon, indicating direction and speed. Such underwater weeds can be added using the sgraffito technique. First lay down a bright green layer of underpainting. Leave it to dry and then paint over the top with a darker green. Then take your brush and, using the end of the handle, scratch the direction of the weeds into the paint so that the bright green shows through.

Indicating the current

Some artists put across the movement of the water through directional brushwork, following the course of the river with strong strokes of the brush or pastel stick. In watercolor, these strokes will be painted dark over light; with opaque media, light over dark. However, you need to be careful to blend them together or it will look like a river of spaghetti. Try to view your river objectively, noticing how the shadows and reflections fall on the water; if you look at the river just as a collection of lines, it can lose its

"wet"qualities and appear solid.

Another way to indicate the speed and direction of the water is to add a few current lines once the painting is finished. With watercolor, you can reserve them initially with liquid frisket, or add them at the end as "highlights" in white gouache. With oils or acrylics, try etching a few sharp strokes into the paint with the end of the brush to reveal the white canvas below, sgraffito-style. With pastels, you may need to fix the painting so that the lines will not merge with the pastel particles in the previous layer (although remember that fixing will darken the tones).

▲ **Where Salmon Leap, River Inver** (oil)
WILLIAM GARFIT
The churning, peat-stained water rushes through gulleys and over rocks, captured by building up layers of color from dark to light. Touches of white add a sparkle to the water.

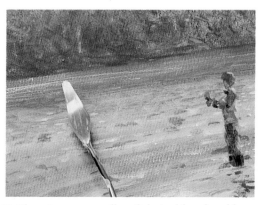

3 *Changing to a small, soft-haired brush, add the boy, and then put in some lighter patches of reflected light on the water. Scrape out more directional lines with a painting knife so that the white canvas shows through.*

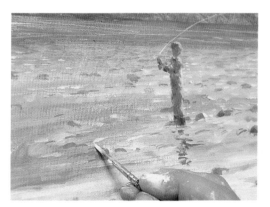

4 *Scrape out the rod with a single, clear stroke, and then add final touches of white highlights. Smudge highlights in the background with a finger to soften and blend them with the color of the water.*

White water

The British artist, David Hockney, commented on the irony of painting *The Bigger Splash*. The split-second effect caused by somebody diving into a swimming pool took him weeks to build up with small, painstaking brushstrokes.

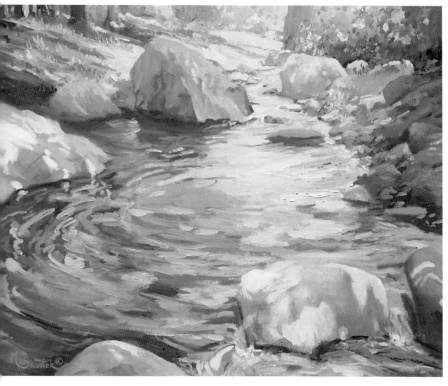

▲ **San Dimas Creek** (oil)

MARTHA SAUDEK

Directional strokes of pure color express the movement of water in this pool.

Some artists, on the other hand, approach moving water with quite the opposite technique and feel obliged to create the energy of such a splash by applying the paint with similar energy, flicking and spattering it into a frenzy. White water is the most obvious evidence of the power of falling water and occurs wherever it meets an obstruction. You will see it in a mountain stream crashing down a hillside, buffeting against rocks or eroded stone banks. Rapids and waterfalls are good examples, too, where the water tumbles down a drop of many feet and then crashes into a pool below.

White water textures

Painting such white water involves capturing the texture of the water, its speed and movement. It is no good catching the flying spray if it looks frozen in time; it needs to look as if it is moving. You need to use techniques favored by the cartoonist to indicate this movement, blurring edges and following the trajectory of a moving object – in this case, the spray.

White water is rather like snow in that it takes on the color of the prevailing light – for example, in the evening it will reflect the pinkness of the evening sunlight. It does not reflect an image like a flat pool of water, but the whiteness reflects back colors such as a blue sky above.

Like snow, too, it has shadows and highlights that are not very easy to identify or capture. As fast-flowing water cascades over the rocks, it breaks up and catches the light,

White Water Techniques: Acrylics

To begin with, areas of the canvas are left bare for the white water, and delicate shadow tones are added in the water with lively strokes. Then the raft is integrated into the boiling white water with drybrush and spattering.

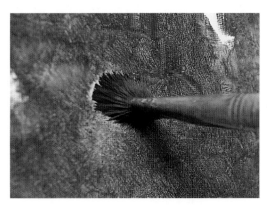

1 *Block in the sheer rocky bank in the background using a coarse brush and a scrubbing motion. As the focus is on the water and raft, this area is left cursorily painted.*

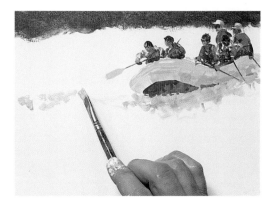

2 *Block in the raft and crew with minimum detail, and then paint in the mid-tone shadows in the water with a pale gray mix. Try to map out the movement in the water using short, lively strokes.*

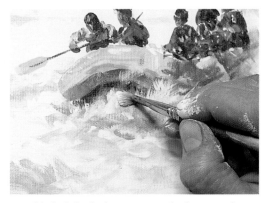

3 *Add slightly darker, greener shadows to the water and then, with a dry brush, drag strokes of undiluted white up over the sides of the buffeted raft.*

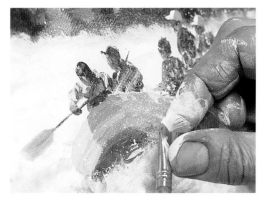

4 *Now charge your brush with dilute white paint and spatter paint over the raft, bending back the bristles and then letting them spring forward to flick out the paint. You will need to experiment with the brush, the dilution of the paint and the distance from the paper as they all affect the spatter.*

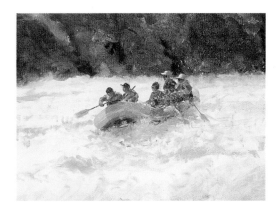

5 *More spattering and drybrush work soften the waterline along the rocks in the background, further describing the turbulence of this white water. There is a real feeling of movement and excitement in this painting.*

White Water Techniques: Watercolor

To start with, white highlights are reserved with liquid frisket and clear wax. Then water shadows are washed over the paper, and darker shadows are added wet-in-wet in the background and wet-on-dry in the foreground. The surrounding landscape is built up from a flat wash in blocks of color wet-in-wet, and more detailed shapes of trees and rocks are superimposed wet-on-dry.

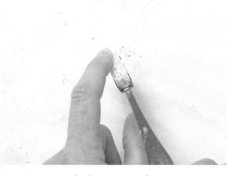

1 *Paint in areas of white water that you want to reserve with liquid frisket. You can spatter some along the bank, too. If you change your mind, you can paint over the reserved paper after you have removed the dried fluid.*

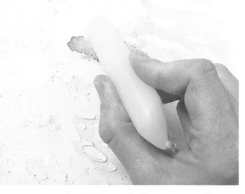

2 *For a softer highlight, rub the paper with a white candle, making broad, directional strokes. Remember that after the wax is laid down, it cannot be removed so that area will have to remain white.*

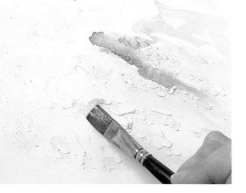

3 *When the liquid frisket is dry, mix a wash of ultramarine, alizarin crimson and Payne's gray, and pick out the shadows in the white water.*

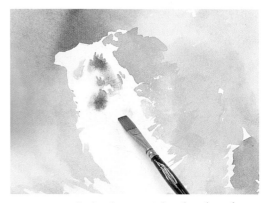

4 *Map out the landscape with colored washes, wet-in-wet, taking care over the detail of the edges between the water and rocky bank. For the rocks and shadows, add color wet-in-wet so that the edges are blurred.*

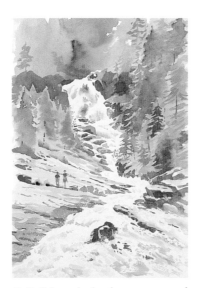

5 *Build up the landscape wet-on-dry and add the dark parts of the rocks. When the paint is quite dry, remove the liquid frisket with a soft kneaded eraser. Finally, add the two figures.*

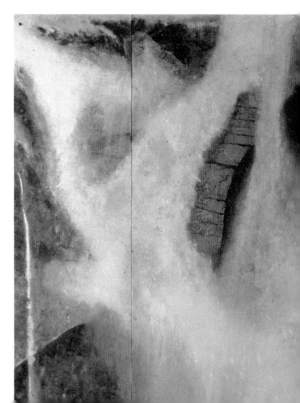

and then disappears into shadow. Remember, too, that the shadows cast by trees or by the bank can be seen particularly clearly when they are cast across white water.

Hard edges

White water is often seen against dark water or landscape elements – such as rocks or a mossy bank – and the contrast between the extremes of light and dark can produce a stark edge. This may emphasize the whiteness of the foam, but it can also make the foam look too solid. It is this kind of detail that you need to look out for when you are standing back from your painting to assess it toward the end.

You may be able to solve the problem by softening the edge. Run your thumb along it if you are working in pastels, or run a torchon, or cotton-tipped stick, backward and forward over the edge so that the two abutting colors are blended together a little. In watercolor, soften the edge by taking a pristine brush and clean water, and running the dampened brush along the edge until the color starts to lift off. Then blot it with a clean tissue. You will have to take care to do this gently or you will damage the paper.

With oils or acrylics you can soften the edge with a brush if the paint is not yet dry.

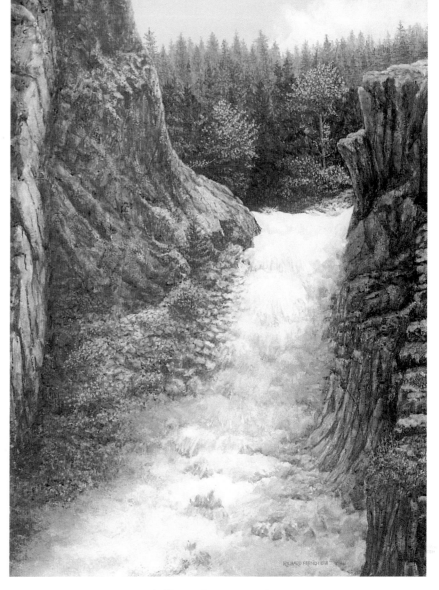

▲ **Cascade** (watercolor on gesso surface)
R. FRENCH
Care is taken with textures in this painting, particularly in the rocks and water. Pale blue shadows are finely stippled in the water and over the landscape along the water's edge with a dry brush. White highlights are then added, leaving the cool blues for the shadow of the rock across the fall.

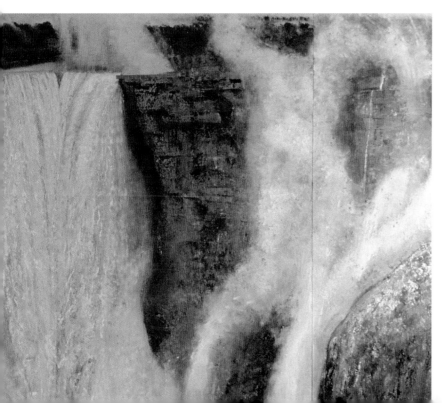

◄ **Falls of Kaieteur, Guyana 1**
(triptych, oil)
KEITH GRANT
In a dramatic view of the power of nature the artist distinguishes between the textures in the cascading water and those in the rising vapor.

Pastel Over Gouache

A dark, mottled base is left to dry, and lively white pastel strokes are used to describe highlights in the white water.

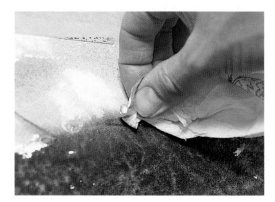

1 *Map out the river with a dark wash of not-too-dilute gray. Before it dries, take some paper towels twisted to a point and stipple them over the paint to give a mottled effect.*

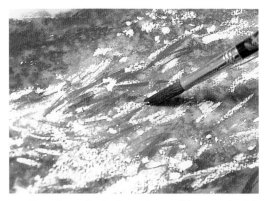

2 *When the paint is dry, take a white pastel stick and work it over the top. Keep the strokes descriptive of the rushing water by making short, lively strokes punctuated with stipples and points, created by twisting the stick on the paper.*

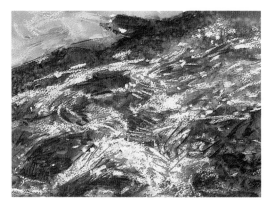

3 *With a dark blue-gray mix, make further painted strokes over the pastel to increase the feeling of movement.*

▼ **Ryuzu Falls, above Lake Chuzenji, Nikko, Japan** (pastel)

ELSIE DINSMORE POPKIN

Working from dark to light, the artist scumbles blue shadows in the falls over the darks, and adds white highlights with short, sharp strokes.

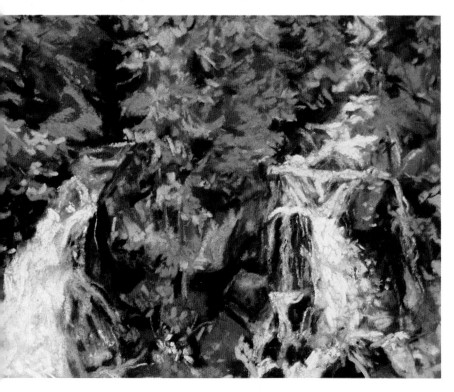

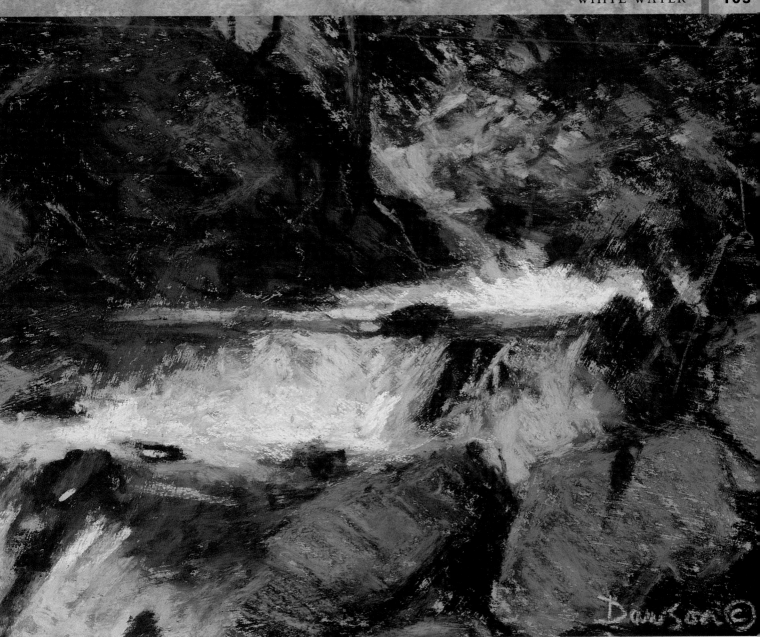

If it is dry, use a dry brush and a very small amount of white paint mixed with a touch of blue to superimpose a softer layer over the foam, blurring the edge a little.

White water techniques

With watercolor you need to reserve the areas of white with liquid frisket, or just by mapping them out at the start, so that you do not paint over them. Texture can be added into these areas as tones of shadow by stippling with a dry brush. You can add specks of spray by stippling white body color with a fine sable brush or by scraping into the white paper with a sharp scalpel.

Oil pastels can be used with turpentine and applied with a brush to produce an impasto effect. For areas of spray, fix the darker background. When this is dry, use a small piece of white pastel on its side to scumble over the top.

With opaque media, you can build up the background, and then add the foam with thick, impasto paint. Apply it with a dry brush or knife, or flick or stipple it. Another technique you could try is to add sand to the white paint to give it more texture.

▲ **A Study of White Water**
(pastel)
DOUG DAWSON
By focusing on a stretch of river, the artist creates a pattern of colors and tones that is semi-abstract. Superimposed, broken strokes capture the drama of the rushing water.

Reflections

Reflections occur on moving water, but their effect is more generalized as the ruffled water breaks up the reflected image, making it less intense in color, and with only a suggestion of the form of the object reflected. You will see only patches of color if sky is reflected in moving water, while on flat parts of a river, the reflection will be clearer and more complete.

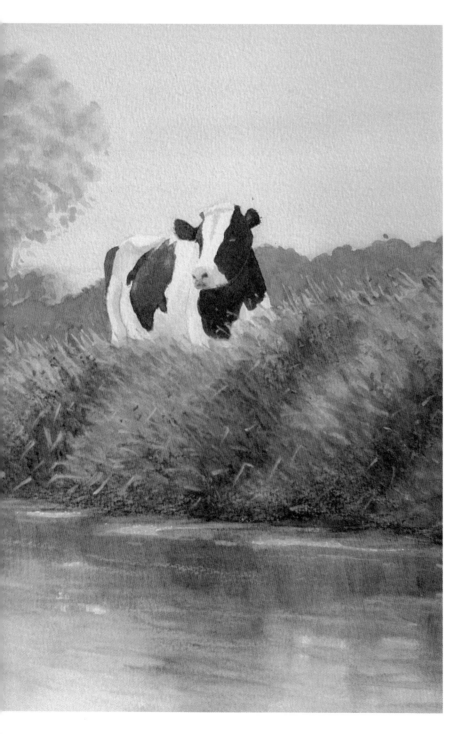

For a reflection to be good and clear, water needs to be flat and transparent – so that, as soon as the surface is ruffled or the water is opaque, the reflections will be fragmented and blurred. As we have discovered, in any moving river you will find a wide variety of different states of water, all of which will reflect in different ways. With experience, you will learn about the relative reflectivity of these different states, though, even after studying water for years, you are often surprised. For instance, a moving river which appears flat does not always reflect as clearly as you might expect. You will find on closer inspection that this is because the surface is a simmering layer of water, which makes it opaque and distorted and does not reflect very well at all.

The fact that reflections are affected by the nature of the water means that you can use them to help describe the changing character of the surface, using repeated patches of reflected color for gentle ripples, clearer reflections for areas of flatter water, and fragments of reflected color in more agitated water.

◄ **Reflective Mood** (watercolor)
BART O'FARRELL
With dull light and broken water, the reflection of the cow is just suggested. Soft drybrush techniques capture the calm water surface.

Unifying the water

A common approach with pastels is to blend the initial layers and then use more graphic, textural strokes toward the end. To unify an area – or if necessary the whole painting – an artist will use repetitive strokes. Here they are used to map out the reflections on the surface of the moving river.

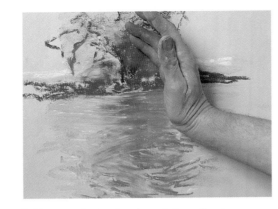

1 *Plot out the landscape and the reflection, blending the dark area of the reflection outward with the side of a hand.*

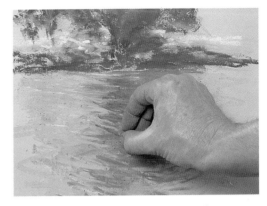

2 *Work darker brown, horizontal strokes over the top of the brown area and into the stone color, making the strokes as crisp as possible.*

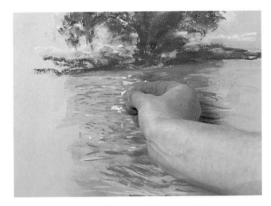

3 *Work in pale yellow strokes over the stone and into the brown. Finally, add points of sparkling highlights.*

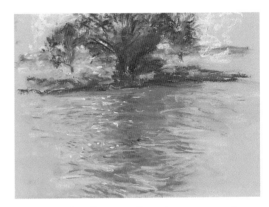

4 *The graphic directional strokes map out the surface of the river, in contrast to the more intuitive strokes of the landscape. They also suggest a moving current in the water.*

▶ **River Ash Series, Summer**
(pastel)
JOHN PLUMB
Reflections distorted by movement in the water are expressed with pale, linear, snake-like marks over a dark base.

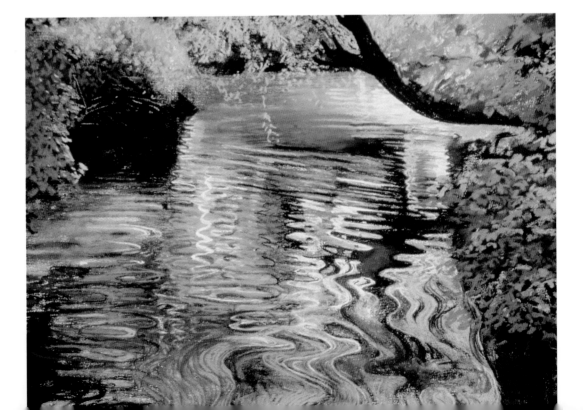

Shadows

Shadows fall across moving water in the same way as still water, creating areas of deeper tone. The strength of the shadows will depend on the light. Strong light creates extremes of tone – dark shadows and bright highlights. Dull days reduce extremes and call for subtle mid-tones. Any movement of the water in the shadow area is likely to reflect light so that areas of dark will be broken by striations of light.

Shadows do not need to be a negative part of your painting – they offer a contrast to the brighter reflections and they should be treated with as much attention as the rest of the painting. The problem begins with thinking of shadows on water as simply dark, flat areas of paint. You will see in the examples on this page different ways of painting shadows. Try building it up with a multitude of colors applied in small strokes to make a shimmering area of shadow. Otherwise, you could try applying the paint unevenly in one layer and superimpose linear marks to map out the surface.

Shadows cast by trees or buildings across a river will be more visible on lighter parts of the water, particularly on white water. With transparent media such as watercolor this is easier to contrive as the shadow can be taken as a colored gray wash over the stretch of river in question, darkening the various tones as it travels across the surface. With opaque media, paint the shadow first, adding the highlights, appropriately subdued, over the top.

▶ **The Horseshoe Bend, River Kennet** (oil)

WILLIAM GARFIT

Dark shadows break up blurred reflections that are weak because the river is cloudy and moving. The main color of the paler reflection is scumbled over the edge of the darker shadow, with details in hatched, horizontal strokes.

▶ **Bridge at St Sevier de Rustar** (pastel)

PATRICK CULLEN

The shadow cast across the water by the bridge is built up with flecks of complementary colours – yellows and magentas, warm browns and blues with touches of darks superimposed over the top. As a result, the shadows create a positive area, generating energy.

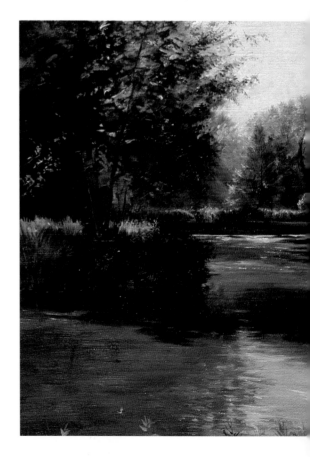

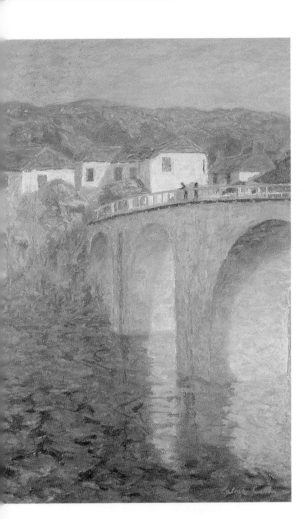

Integrating Shadows and Reflections

Using oils, block in the landscape, keeping it simple. Place the dark green shadows and reflections first and then add the sky reflections. Finally, work on the surface of the river to distinguish it from the land and indicate movement.

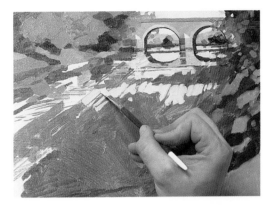

1 *Build up the landscape adding the tree shadow and foliage reflections along the bank. Apply paint unevenly, in all directions, adding directional strokes for the river.*

2 *Put in the sky, and cut in the sky reflections around the shadows and reflections in the water. Take the blue over the shadow edges to integrate the two colors.*

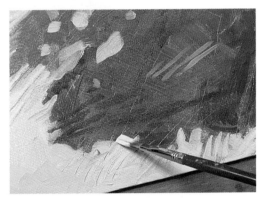

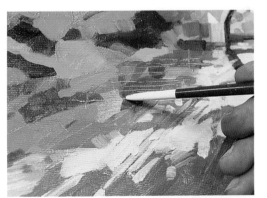

3 *Using the end of the brush, scrape lines into the paint to reveal the canvas and establish the surface of the water where the foliage reflections rest.*

4 *Add darker strokes of green closer to the bank to suggest the depths of the water, which would be visible through the surface shadow.*

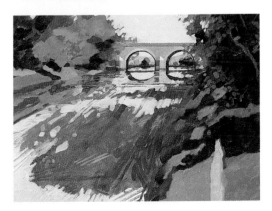

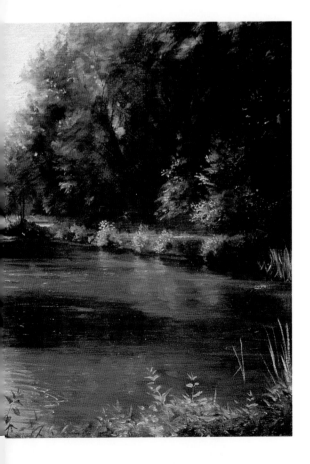

Color

Like all bodies of water, rivers take on the color of their surroundings. Yet the water sometimes has a color of its own. You will probably have seen mountain streams almost red from deposits of iron and peat, making any churning "white" water look a rich creamy color. Fast-moving rivers, particularly if they are swollen with flood water, can carry along silt and rubbish that make them opaque and murky. Large city rivers are often dark with dirt. Yet take a glass of water from any of these rivers and it will appear transparent. Only a closer look will reveal the deposits that give it its overall color.

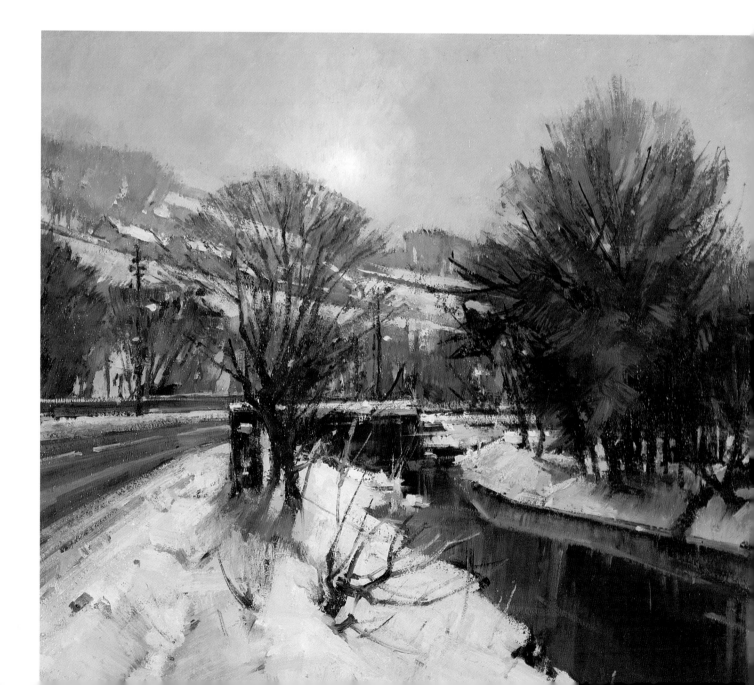

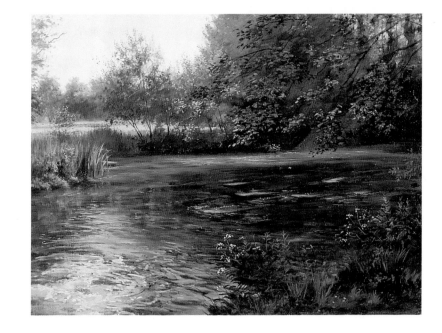

◄ **Mill Pool at Itchen Abbas, River Itchen** (oil)
WILLIAM GARFIT
The "color" of a river is influenced by reflections, light, and shade, as well as by the depth, state, and clarity of the water. In addition, in this scene green patches of weed color the depths and interrupt the surface.

▼ **Winter Sun, Delph** (oil)
JOHN McCOMBS
In the dying light of a winter evening, the river cuts through the contrasting snow like a black chasm. Pale reflections are scumbled over the dark underlying color.

Even if you can isolate the overall color of a particular river, your painting will look unconvincing if you leave it at that. The overall color can be used as a base in the underpainting or repeated here and there across the whole area of water. However, like still water, a river is never a single, flat color but a mass of colors and tones made up of reflections, shadows and river vegetation, distorted and churned by the movement of the river itself.

Color does not exist without light, so naturally light affects the perceived colors of a river. Dull light reduces a body of water to a dark chasm that can be used to cut dramatically into and across the picture space. Bright light, on the other hand, reveals variations in color and tone – areas of pure color caused by reflected light from the sky, patches of dark shadows and golden sunlight.

Sketches and underpainting

Try some quick sketches, mapping out the tones in charcoal, and exploring the color with conté pencils or pastels. Once you have decided on the approach, develop the composition. If you are using oils or acrylics, you can map out the composition, or retrace your sketch if you started with one, using local colors in order to get a better idea of the final painting. Use dilute paint and broad strokes to avoid too much detail. If you are using watercolors, you can cover the area with pale, wet-in-wet washes, taking care to reserve areas of white, and then map out the general blocks of color and tone.

Other approaches

The colors of a reflection fragmented by turbulence or where a river bed can be seen through the clear water are difficult to reproduce. With opaque mediums, simplify the profusion of colors and tones by laying down a body of dark, blended color to suggest murky depths and work over it with graphic strokes of pure color. With pastels, blend colors over the water area and superimpose lively, paler strokes to follow the movement of the water and pick out the fragmented light. With oils, work wet-in-wet, building up from a darker base, plotting the pattern of color on the water's surface with carefully placed strokes. As acrylics dry very fast, you have the opportunity to use dry-brush techniques as well as wet-in-wet in one sitting.

With watercolors, reserve patches of highlight, mapping them out with a pencil or blocking them with liquid frisket or wax. Lay down the mid-tone colors wet-in-wet and then superimpose darks wet-on-dry.

Harmonizing diversity

You will need to take care, when combining widely different techniques across one stretch of water, that the resulting painting does not appear dislocated. You can prevent this when using opaque media by working over an underpainting done in the water's overall color. Patches of underpainting showing through at intervals will hold the area of water together. Lay a thin red/brown ground over the water area, and when it is dry, work the various techniques over the top letting points of the underpainting show through.

▼ **Nichol Hole, Evening, River Eden** (oil)
WILLIAM GARFIT
The golden, evening light unifies this painting. The water has its own unity, however, due to the use of small, horizontal strokes that express the areas of reflected light.

Just as underpainting creates a sense of harmony, deliberate use of repetitive colors across the area of water will unite the painting. For example, if you are working on an area of reflected blue sky, add touches of the same color here and there across the rest of the water. The eye will naturally follow such a pathway. This technique will be more effective if you use colors that come forward in the painting – colors mixed with warmer reds and yellows.

It is important to build up the whole area of water at the same time, not allowing yourself to work up some dramatic white water and neglect a more boring cluster of rocks. Working in this way, you will be giving this area of diversity some cohesion.

Repetitive techniques

If you have built up the various layers of underpainting together, you can then afford to be more expressive in the last stages. This is a common approach with pastels where the first applications of color are blended and descriptive detail is added in a more

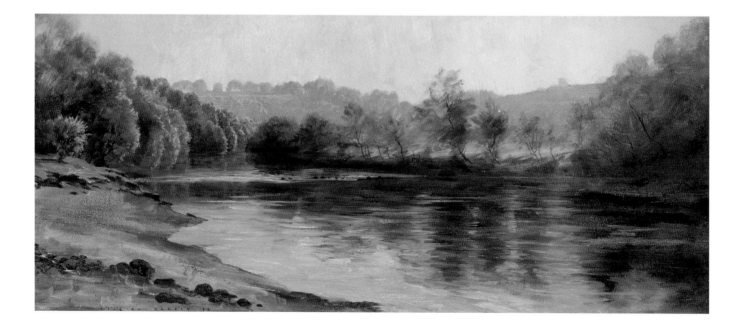

graphic manner toward the end.

Any repetitive technique will help to pull together the diversity of the river water – repeated hatching strokes, feathering, or stippling. These are often suggested by the behavior of the water itself where the light catches ripples at different stages down the river or the water boils up into a patch of white water. Such areas will catch the eye and cause it to travel the length of the river.

Repetitive brushstrokes across the area of water will also help to unite the painting, even if they are interrupted by descriptive passages of a more turbulent nature.

▶ **After the Rain**
(oil)
MARTHA SAUDEK
Capturing the up-tempo clarity after a cleansing rainstorm, the artist plots the course of the stream with touches of reflected blue sky – colder in the background than in the foreground. The blue is picked out on the tree trunks, in the shadows of the rocks, and in the background tree shadows.

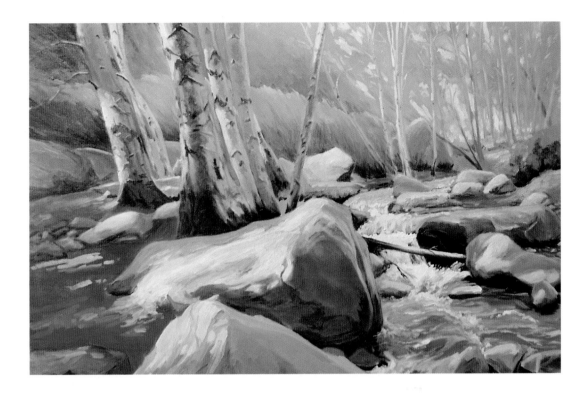

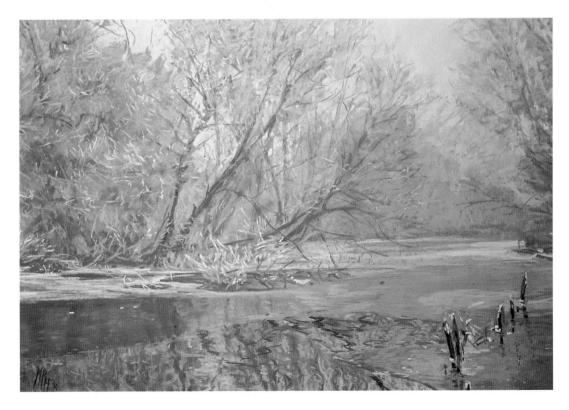

◀ **Frost at Flatford** (pastel)
MARGARET GLASS
In this frosty scene, pale, delicate tones of color – pinks, blues and yellows – are superimposed over a warm, mid-tone tinted paper, which can be seen in tiny patches through the broken pastel strokes at all stages along the river.

The changing nature of the river

If 20 artists painted the same stretch of river, you would be surprised by the different interpretations and extremes of mood that would result. This is one of the joys of painting water. It is a very expressive subject that lets artists give full vent to their emotions. The disadvantage is that the variety of information on a particular stretch of water can be overwhelming, and a painting can end up being so confused that it says nothing.

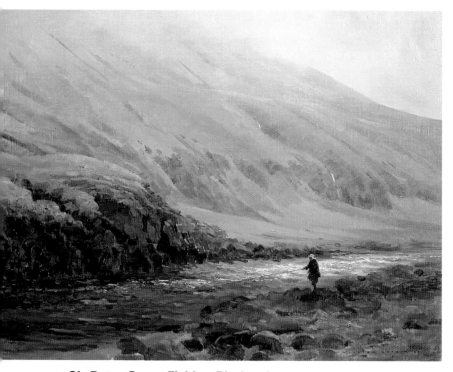

▲ **Sir Peter Green Fishing Birches in the Rain, River Hofsa** (oil)

WILLIAM GARFIT

The artist sees the river as part of a natural force that dwarfs humankind, so he stands back, placing the lone fisherman within the panorama.

The problem of reducing the mass of visual information presented in a river scene down to manageable proportions is a common one for artists. It will help you to decide what it is that you are trying to put across in your painting before you start. This may require a few moments of intense concentration, but it is well worth the time and energy, and will genuinely simplify the painting process in the long run. Ask yourself some questions about the subject. Is it the speed and drama of the water that attracts you? If so, concentrate on describing areas of white water, contrasting them with slow passages, to put your point across. You would in this case need to choose a time of the day when these aspects of the river are shown at their best – that is, when the light is strong to show up the contrasts.

If, however, you want to capture a sense of peace and harmony with nature that is evoked by bubbling water, you might portray the same river in a different light – literally. You might choose a time of day with a softer light that casts shadows of the

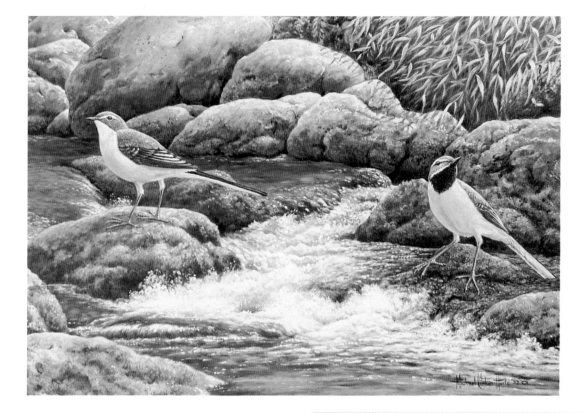

◄ **Grey Wagtails**
(acrylic)
MICHAEL KITCHEN-
HURLE
*To show these birds
in their natural
habitat it is necessary
to focus in on the
bubbling stream.*

surrounding trees across the river. The water itself would pull the composition together but would not be the only focus.

Using props

Human activity on a river can change the way we perceive it, so you might consider including a prop in your painting to build on the mood you are trying to create. A view of a lone fisherman casting across a river will produce a different reaction to a painting of the same river with a young couple in a punt, or with a crowd in a river taxi motoring by. The fisherman would suggest peace and solitude, and a sense of time standing still. The punting couple would introduce a more romantic, secret view of the river, whereas the river taxi would immediately put across a sense of speed, journeying, and a reminder that life was going on somewhere else, too.

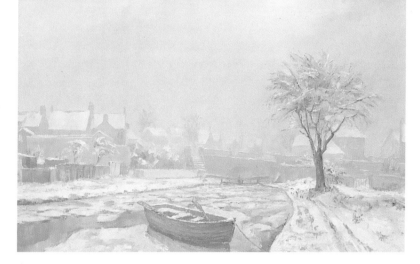

▲ **Ice on the
Canal** (oil)
BRIAN BENNETT
*Painting with a
knife, the artist
emphasizes the cold
with cool blues.*

Rivers through the seasons

If you have a chance to study a river, stream or brook through the seasons, you will see considerable changes in its character during the year. It is not only the water itself that changes, reflecting a drought or thaw, but the prominence of the river in its surroundings also fluctuates. This applies both to a city river and one in dense woodland, though changes in nature, and particularly in the weather, obviously affect the latter more.

Such nuances in our everyday life often go undetected, and the best way to compare the variations through the seasons is regularly to sketch or photograph the same stretch of river. In a river running through woodland, the contrast between summer and winter will be great. In summer the foliage will obscure parts of the river from the sky. The shadows will be deep, and during a hot summer the water will be sluggish. In winter, more of the water surface will be visible and, on a cold but bright winter's day, it will shine like a silver snake, reflecting the sky. Fall colors are always a pleasure to paint, as the symphony of reds, yellows, and browns in the landscape is reflected in the river.

The seasons are never so obvious in the city, where nature has been ousted by brick and concrete, but if you choose to study a river in urban surroundings you will see how changes in the quality of the light throughout the year affect the appearance of the water.

With snow on the ground, the water in stream will appear very dark in the shadows. With opaque media, build up this color with a number of loosely painted layers so that

▶ **Twilight's Last Gleaming**
(watercolor)
ROLAND ROYCRAFT
Washes are superimposed one over another to build tone, with white paper reserved for highlights. A pink light filters through the misty trees, warming the reflections on snow and water.

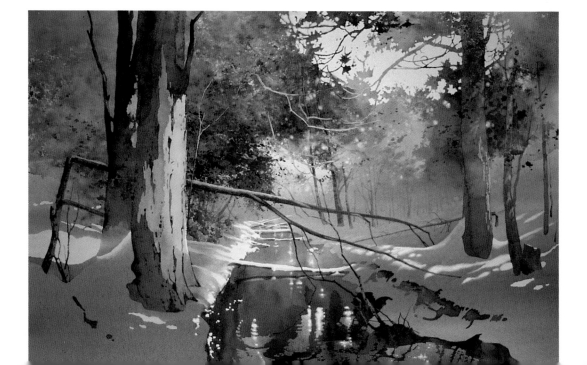

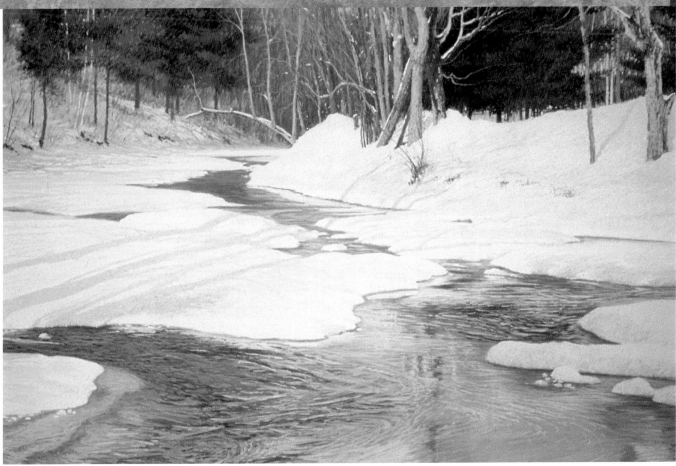

▲ **The White River** (soft pastel on sanded paper)

NEIL DREVITSON

The emphasis is on icy-cold blues reflected in the river and found in the shadows cast on the snow.

▼ **Summer Thames** (oil)

PAUL KENNY

As the summer turns to fall, the artist has emphasized the change of season with rich golds and reds.

the colors mix optically to create a depth of color. Snow appears to freeze all movement, so running water in a stream will contrast nicely with its surroundings. White water will appear dirty compared with the snow. Work with whites tinted with yellow for water in spate, and with white touched with blue for the snow.

Cooling the temperature

For a cold scene, emphasize the cool colors. These are hues on the color wheel that are closer to blue; for example, mix colors from a blue-yellow (such as lemon yellow) rather than a red-yellow (cadmium red). Blue itself can be cold or warm: cobalt is cooler than ultramarine blue, but ultramarine can be cooled with a touch of lemon yellow. If you deliberately gear colors to the cooler part of the color wheel, you will be able to put across the cool temperature of the scene. Take cool blues and browns right across the painting to emphasize the temperature.

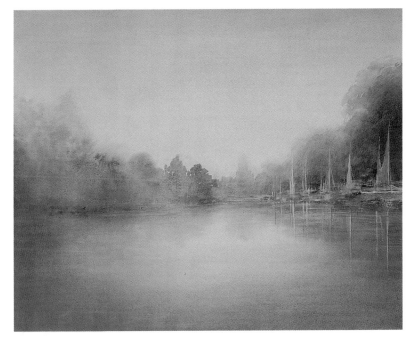

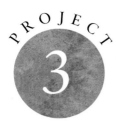
Expressionistic Water

The drama of leaping salmon pitting their strength against a seething mass of falling water is captured here in watercolor with every expressive technique mustered to put across the conflicting forces. The painting works because, although it uses expressive techniques, the structure of the composition is carefully considered on the way, such as the tension between the competing forces, tonal balance and the use of counterchange, where dark marks on bright are matched with the opposite.

Materials used

**140 watercolor paper
(16 × 12 inches)**

●

Watercolor paints: French ultramarine blue, cerulean blue, alizarin crimson, yellow ocher, burnt umber.

●

Brushes: ½" flat, large soft round sable watercolor sizes 0, 2 and 12.

●

Liquid frisket

●

Round-ended palette knife

●

Paper towels

●

Pencils

●

Eraser

●

White chalk

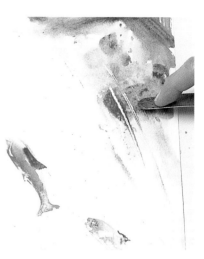

1 *First, reserve the splashes of white with liquid frisket applied with the brushend to save the brush. These splashes are not visible at this stage but will be seen in the final picture. When dry, background rocks and the salmon are added in grays and blue, wet-in-wet and then splashes are taken out with a round-ended knife.*

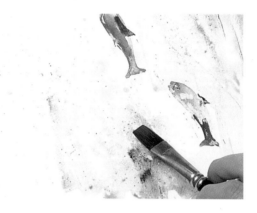

2 *The blue and gray of the body of water is added. Painting in the salmon early on helps you to judge the compositional forces in the picture.*

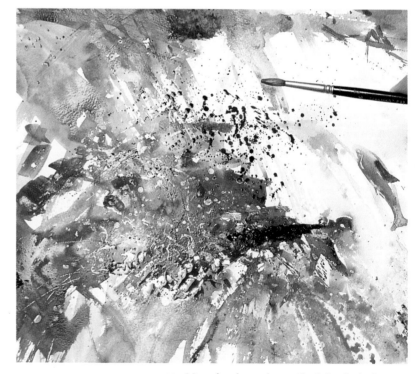

3 *Now for the rocks on the left which are indicated with stronger color and tone – rich brown and an intense blue. Now lighter browns and blues are added around the focal hiatus with strong directional strokes emphasizing the downward movement of the water.*

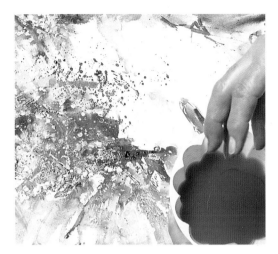

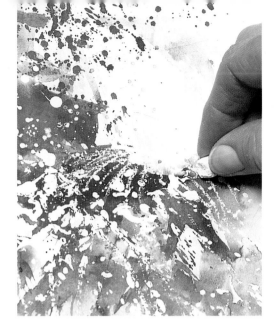

5 *When the painting is dry, the liquid frisket is removed with a clean finger or eraser. The artist chose to emphasize the downward force of the water with directional strokes of white chalk, broken by the texture of the paper.*

4 To add a counterchange to the white splashes, dark gray is flicked with the brush. Then, with the fingers, another level of tone is flicked across, using the neutral mix from the water bowl.

▼ **Leaping Salmon**

KAY OHSTEN

The dark splashes take the eye diagonally across the picture space encouraging further exploration and offering a counter to the diagonal bands of tone.

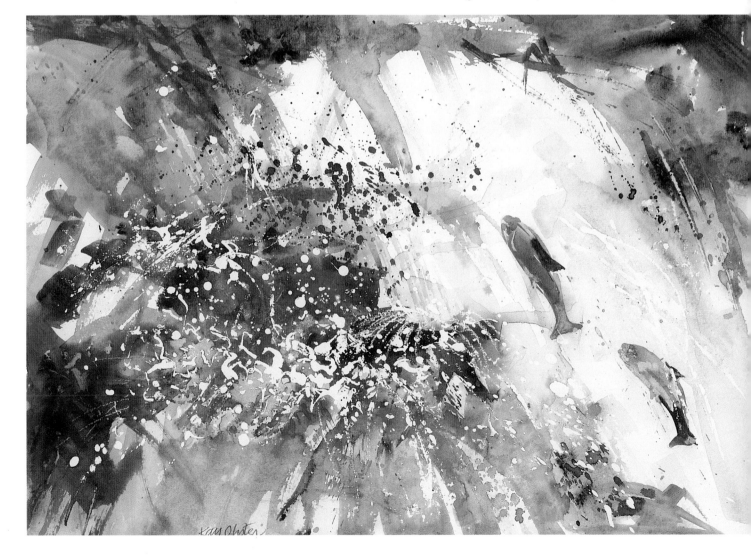

PROJECT 4

Study of Summer River

With a careful study of the dynamics of the composition as the foundation of the painting, the paint is applied precisely, keeping the strokes fresh and clear. Painted in one sitting, the depth achieved relies on the early attention to rich translucent darks – warm burnt umber combined with cooler viridian and French ultramarine. Building up from thin dilute layers to thicker applications, scumbled dryly or applied juicily to catch the light, the result captures the varying depths of a flowing river with all the tricks that light can play on it.

Materials used

Oil paints: flake white, lemon yellow, cadmium yellow, yellow ocher, light red, burnt umber, alizarin crimson, cerulean blue, French ultramarine, viridian green, lamp black.

●

Canvas board

●

Brushes: worn, small flat sable; No 2 round hog; Nos 1 and 3 short flat hogs

●

Mixing palette

●

Turpentine

●

Palette knife

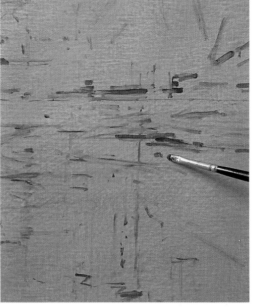

1 Give the canvas board a fairly thick layer of oil primer applied so that the brushmarks show. When dry, apply a thin layer of burnt umber and leave it to dry for a week. With a thin wash of black, map out the horizontals balanced with verticals, and some diagonals, too.

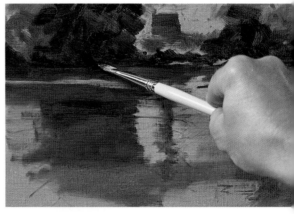

2 With a larger flat hogshair brush, start feeling for the darks using mostly burnt umber with viridian, diluted with turpentine. Keep the water strokes horizontal and the darks rich – don't add any white.

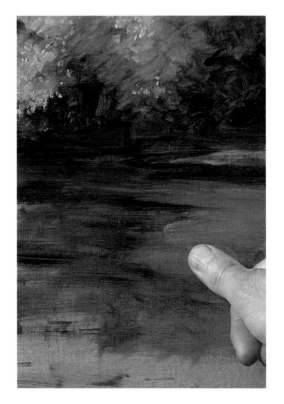

3 Build up the foliage on the bank with general thin glazes of green and thicker impasto touches for the sunlit leaves. Keep building up the greens, applying paint more thickly now and rubbing it into the canvas with your thumb to keep this layer smooth.

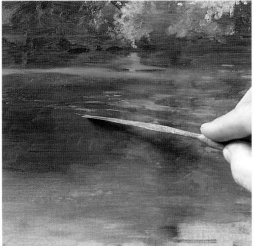

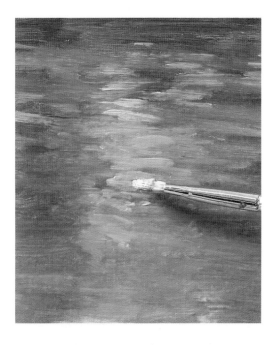

5 Now add thicker strokes of paler blue-green so that the light catches the edge of the physical stroke, to help the illusion of moving, sparkling light which is a flowing river.

4 Having added a blue pathway reflected from the sky with the thicker paint scumbled in a broken stroke over the top, take touches into the foliage. Now with the edge of a palette knife, take this blue over the rich darks as if the light were catching the current. Let the knife scrape back the dark paint, too.

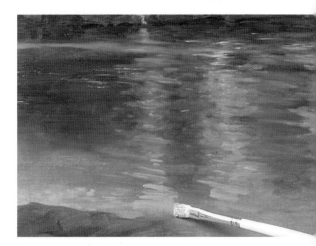

7 Tidy up the foreground, adding a suggestion of a bank and continuing the highlights down to join it. The paler umber wash still visible through the early thin layers suggests shallower water closer in.

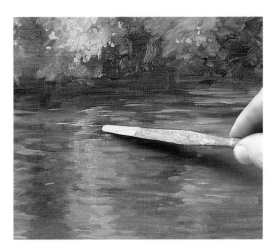

6 Using the knife again, scrape back the paint to the underpainting for glints of light where the reflection is strongest closest to the source. Add touches of paler green as highlights down the reflection.

▶ **Summer Flowing River**
WILLIAM GARFIT
Final touches of warm highlights are added, the brushstroke breaking the warm white with the underlying paint so it is not too bright.

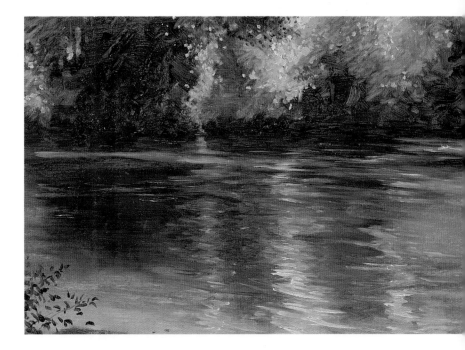

The sea

It is no wonder that painters have always been fascinated by the sea. It draws you to it – thrilling you one moment with murderous explosions of spray and charming you the next with a gentle, musical lapping sound. This unpredictability makes it an enthralling subject and provides an in-built sense of tension. These moods, too, are useful to the artist in the way that they reflect aspects of human nature.

The sea can be approached from many different angles: by recording the lives of those who live and work near and on it, and deal with it daily in its many forms, ugly and divine. It can be painted as a playground for holidays and sport, a place of pleasure. And then there is the sea alone – in its natural state, as part of nature, as a habitat for birds, fish and marine life, integrated with rocks, cliffs, bays, lagoons, and secret islands.

As with rivers, one of the challenges of painting the sea lies in capturing the impression of water on the move – tidal water, currents, waves and eddies. Waves, particularly, repay prolonged study as it is all too easy for the artist to work to a formula.

There are very many ways of painting the sea. Books on the history of art illustrate how different the approaches and techniques have

▼ **Start of Summer** (oil)
DENISE BURNS
Capturing the joys of summer, the artist paints the reflections on the wet sand with a masterful display of enervated brushstrokes.

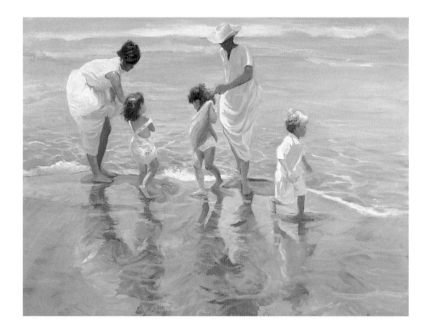

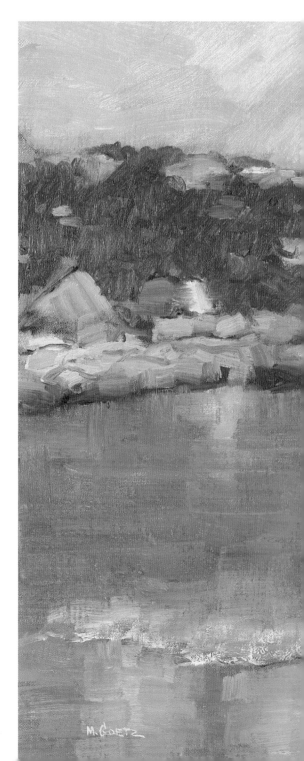

been. The craftsmen of Ancient Greece painted the sea onto vases and incized it in stone as a backcloth to tales of battles and legends. For the Chinese, and then the Japanese, the sea was a subject in itself, painted as part of their eulogy to nature. Certain artists have excelled in capturing the spirit of the sea, such as the American Winslow Homer (1836–1910), with his watercolor paintings of Bermudan life – the sea translucent and blue, and then whisked to a boiling cauldron.

Influenced by the Impressionists, the Spanish painter, Joaquin Sorolla y Bastida (1863–1923), produced paintings that captured the essence of the sea close to Valencia. However, although an inspiration, the work of these artists should never be slavishly copied. The sea is an emotive subject calling for a personal approach through your own combination of viewpoint, tools and materials, techniques, and style to enable you to produce personal and original statements.

▼ **Rockport Beach**
(oil on linen)
MARY ANN GOETZ
This seaside scene is painted over a warm, brown-tinted canvas, which imbues the painting with a golden evening light.

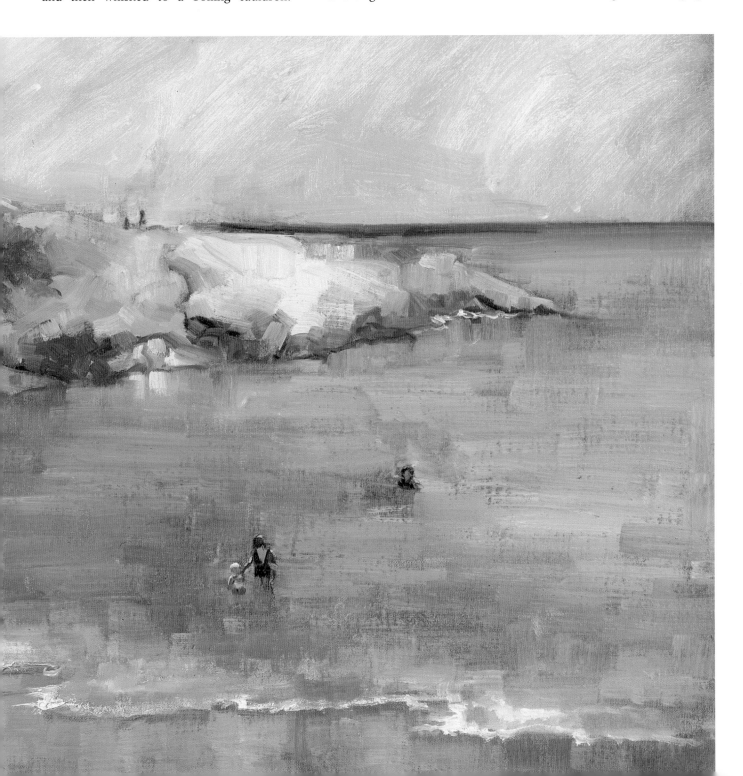

Photo ideas

There are so many different faces to the sea depending on the weather and the light. These photographs are meant to give you some ideas and to help you see what a moving mass of water looks like caught in one split second. Now all you have to do is interpret the scene as it talks to you.

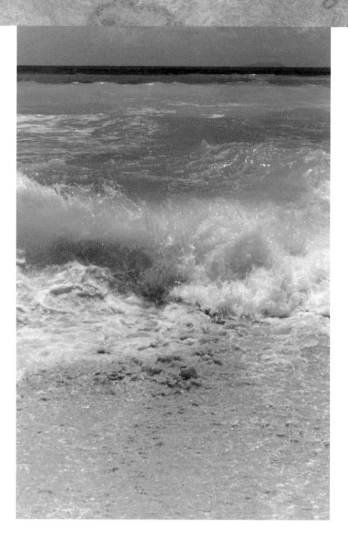

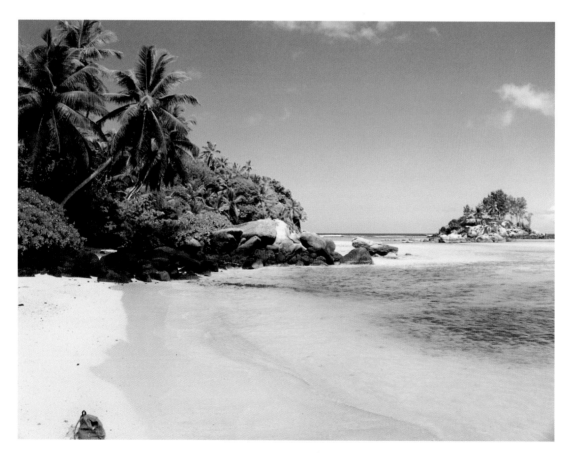

▲ **Breaking Wave, Seychelles**
You could use this for a study, or as part of a larger composition. Try painting it in different styles and different media – abstracted and hard-edged in acrylics, or in soft watercolor washes.

◄ **Tropical Beach, Seychelles**
An inviting coral cove – almost too perfect to be true. Turn to pages 138–139 to see how you can interpret it in watercolor.

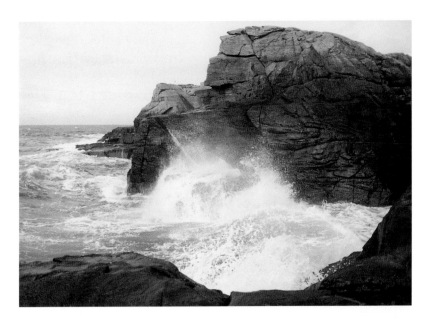

◄ **Coast, Northwest Scotland**

A useful photograph to help you remember the physical formation of breaking waves but there is no drama in the light or the view. Try upping the tempo with brighter colors and more extreme contrasts.

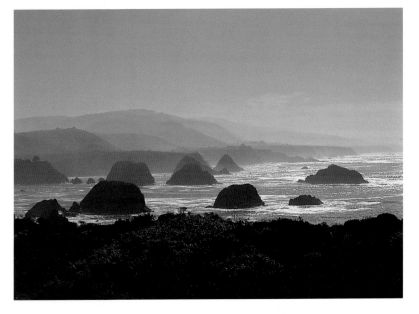

▶ **Near Elk, California**

A dramatic photograph with the composition and tempo carefully considered. The artist can learn from this and it would make a good exercise to copy it. Try painting it in watercolor, reserving the highlights first with liquid frisket.

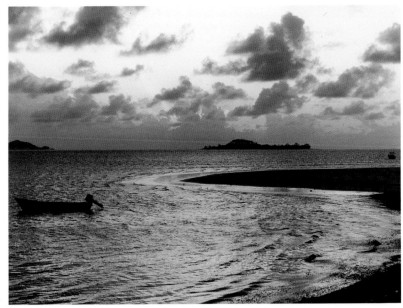

◄ **Evening Shore, Seychelles**

Most cameras will not pick out subtle colors and tones in the evening light, leaving shadows flat and black and highlights starkly white. Pick up on the pinky light, and build up the shadows with thin colored washes or glazes.

Choosing a viewpoint

As with all painting, your choice of viewpoint for a seascape is very important, affecting not only the composition, but also the mood of your painting. When choosing a viewpoint, you will also be choosing where to place the horizon: whether to divide the space between sea and sky or concentrate more on the waves.

Choosing a Viewpoint

Your choice of viewpoint will affect the message that the picture conveys.

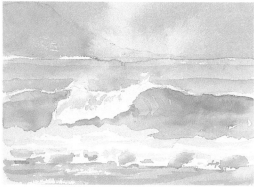

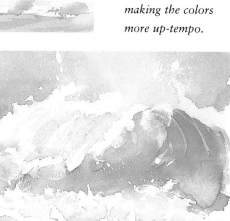

1 A well-balanced view of a breaking wave can be used to show mastery of your medium, but little more. Build the mood by working on the sky and making the colors more up-tempo.

2 By coming close in on the breaking wave, you immediately involve the viewer in the sense of drama and tension that people feel when facing the forces of nature.

3 A bird's-eye view reduces the foreshore to a two-dimensional scheme of pattern and color – abstract at a distance but comprehensible as a landscape from closer in.

The artist looking for an original composition will be affected by the choice of viewpoint. This can be achieved with extremes – a very high, low, close or distant viewpoint – or by an offbeat approach. The painting, above right, not only chooses a high viewpoint, exaggerated by the extreme verticality of the frame shape, but it is also viewed from a distance which suggests the artist was in a plane or on the top of a ferris wheel.

With a high viewpoint, looking down on the sea, the horizon should be placed high in the composition as a large expanse of sea will be visible. This viewpoint flattens out waves, while with a low viewpoint, close to the water's edge, any breaking waves will appear to break over you. The outline of the crest of the closest wave and the tips of those beyond will be seen against the sky, making their three-dimensional form more obvious. This is a technical challenge for any artist.

Focus

When you find a seascape that inspires you to paint it, take time to explore the possibilities, sketching, or just looking through your hands or the viewfinder of your camera. Move around, trying different viewpoints, standing up, sitting down or looking at it obliquely from the side.

The focus of your painting is dictated, to a certain degree, by the weather. If a storm is raging and rain reduces visibility, you may want to focus in on the crashing waves. With a high viewpoint you will lose the vertical height of the waves and surf, and, if you

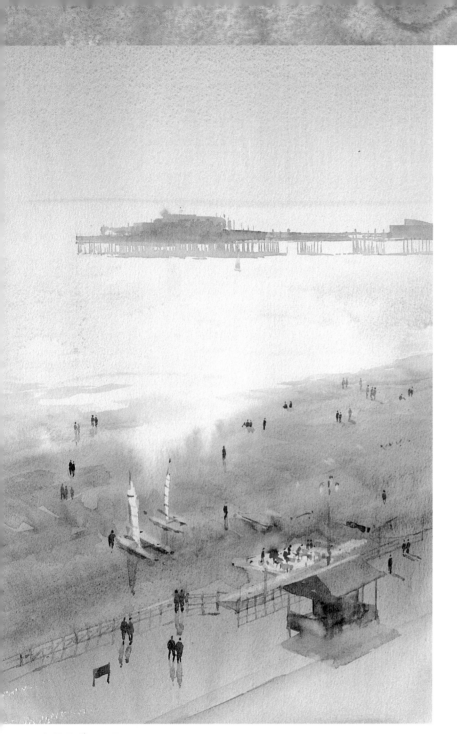

come in too close and too low, you will sacrifice the dramatic potential of the sky and rain.

The artist of the painting, below right, resisted a broader view of the sunset and focused in, with a high, close viewpoint, on the effect of evening light on the water broken by patches of reeds.

Harmony

The division of the picture by the horizon has always concerned artists. Classical teaching dictates that to achieve harmonious relationships between unequal parts of a whole (that is, the area of sea/land and the area of sky), the smaller should be in the same proportion to the larger as the larger is to the whole (that is, the whole picture area). Roughly speaking, study 1, left, shows such a division of the canvas by the horizon. However, you may prefer to express disharmony, seeking out divisions of the picture area which disconcert the viewer instead.

▲ **Brighton Beach** (watercolor)

ALAN OLIVER

This unusual bird's-eye view captures the full panorama of this famous beach with the pier in the background.

▶ **Alameda Beach** (pastel on sandpaper)

KITTY WALLIS

The quality of the evening light and the translucence of the aquamarine water work on the soul, providing food for thought.

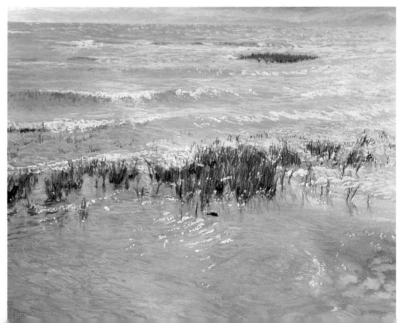

Scale

Many artists are drawn to the sea because of its infinite scale. It offers an opportunity to measure man against the overwhelming vastness and power of nature, reminding us of our insignificance in the scale of the universe. Artists in a seascape strive to capture this sense of the infinite through contrast, a sense of recession, and the use of color.

Vastness can be put across in paintings only by giving the viewer clues to set the scale. An expanse of sea appears infinite only if it is contrasted with something small, such as a fishing boat in the distance, or a tiny figure paddling in the foreground.

A good example of using elements in the composition to set the scale is the famous woodblock print of the curling wave, *The Great Wave off Kanasawa*, by Katsushika Hokusai (1760–1849). It is actually one of thirty-six views of Mount Fuji, which can be seen, on closer inspection, in the distance, though it can be overlooked initially because of the power of the main image. Hokusai's wave looks big, even at first glance, but its monumental size is only confirmed when you spot the skiffs almost consumed in its depths.

Likewise the atmospheric paintings of J.M.W. Turner (1775–1851) of the sea in various extremes of weather – fog, mist, darkness, or snow, often in combination – always include a boat of some sort to act as a focus and to set the scale.

Clues to scale

To set the scale, you need to compare it with an element of a known size. The human figure, and wildlife are obvious candidates as are boats and buoys. Seabirds are often used as unobtrusive clues to the scale of a seascape. They can be hidden wheeling and diving amongst the waves, only visible when you take a more careful look. Finding such a hidden clue to the scale sometimes forces you to reassess the scale of the painting, adding an element of surprise.

More often the artist will want you to discover his clues to the scale of his seascape and will lead you to them through compositional elements, counterchange, or with color. The eye can be led with various tricks involving strong compositional lines along which your eye travels. Patches of bright color or tone, or white wave crests draw the eye across the surface and into the picture space, finally arriving at the destination of the all important clue.

With counterchange, these clues – birds, buoys or boats – will stand out because they will be painted as dark when set against a pale background and light against a dark

▼ **Biscay Rising**
(watercolor)
HAZEL SOAN
All good sailors are apprehensive of the Bay of Biscay, aptly recorded in this brooding study. Just to confirm the alarming size of these threatening waves, the artist sets the scale with the wheeling gulls.

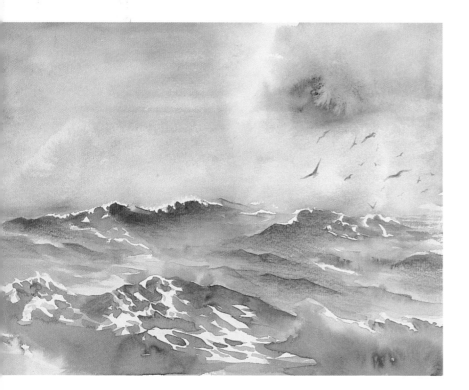

background. Or the artist will emphasize the clue with contrasting color, maybe even a complementary color so that a mere speck will sizzle within the composition – orange against blues, yellow against violets.

A sense of scale

A suggestion of infinite distance in a seascape can also be made without offering clues to the scale, relying on the composition, distribution of color and tone, and a general mood to suggest infinite depths. Try your hand at such a seascape, reducing shapes down to their essentials, casting aside realism and seeking out the mood of the scene with color and expressive techniques. Use compositional lines and textures in the paint as well as suggestions of light to take the eye deep into the picture space.

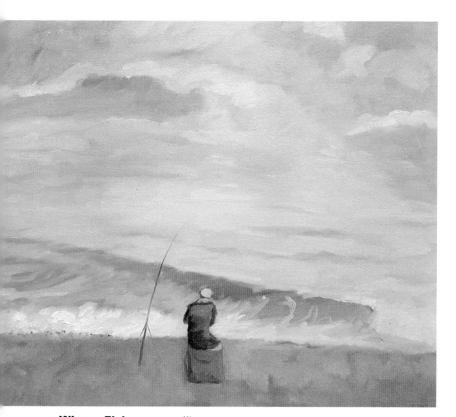

▲ **Winter Fisherman** (oil)

BRIAN YALE

The cold, hunched figure of the lone fisherman sets the scale and gives vertical relief to the horizontality of the composition.

▶ **Distant Summer Sea** (acrylic and sand on board)

ROBERT TILLING

In this understated yet emotive view out to sea, the eye is carried into the picture with a carefully constructed network of diagonals in the foreground and horizontal lines of light in the background. With no element to fix the scale, it appears to stretch to infinity.

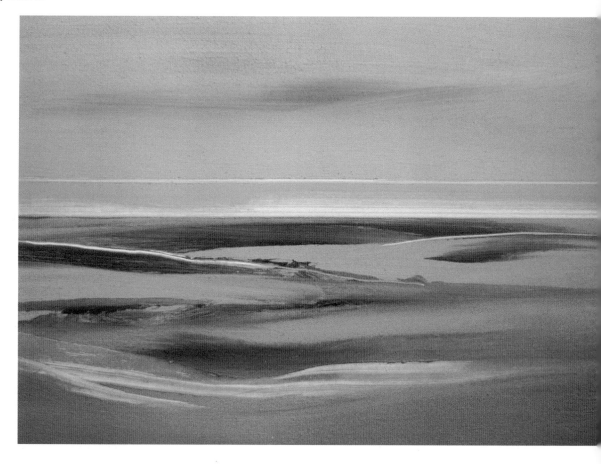

The behavior of waves

Waves come in and break against the shore with hypnotic regularity. Yet at the same time they are all so different. Try sketching their shapes, remembering that they are moving, three-dimensional forms topped by a crest where the water is thinner. The light shines through the crest, giving it a greenish glint. The wave then curls over, casting shadow onto the underside, where it breaks into bright white spume. This then flattens out and is broken into a pattern of white over the darker blue-green of the underlying color.

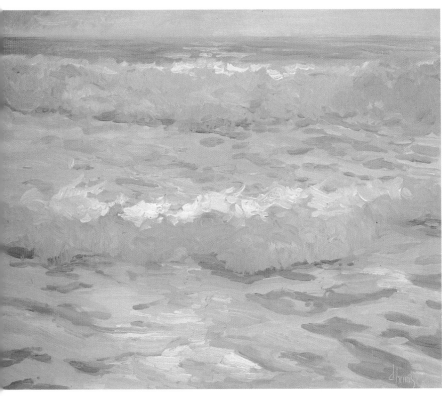

▲ **California's Gold** (oil)

DENISE BURNS

With the setting sun beyond the surf, the light catches the tops of the waves while their leading edges are in shadow, with patches of deeper shadow under the rolling surf.

Sketching from a beach, you may see sand, then a stretch of wet sand reflecting the sky, over which the last wave is just receding, then an area of flat water with the dissolving foam of the last wave, then the nearest, largest wave about to break, with successive rows of waves beyond it. Try painting such a seashore several times, in light that differs in quality and direction. When waves are backlit, the light catches the tops of the waves, emphasizing their edges. When the light is behind you, the contrasts between the foam and the shadows it casts on a wave are brought out. Soft evening light, with the setting sun reflected in the water, is often painted, probably because it is a situation in which many people would like to be suspended *ad infinitum*.

Perspective and waves

Many artists have trouble making seascapes look as though they stretch into infinity rather than climbing relentlessly up hill. To give the impression of distance, emphasize what is there but sometimes difficult to spot – that is, the effect of aerial perspective. This build-up of particles in the atmosphere over distance affects detail, color and tonal value. Waves toward the horizon appear to flatten out, and seem bluer and paler.

Recession

This oil study of a view out to sea uses aerial perspective and a staggered, three-band composition to take the eye into the picture space. The eye glides over the foreground stretch of sand to the breaking waves in the middle ground, which is enlivened with touches of pure color and tonal extremes, and then on into the distant area of less defined water.

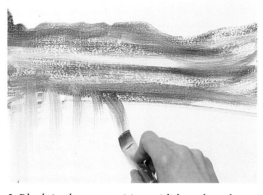

1 *Block in the composition with broad strokes of dilute paint. The three-band design, together with the diminution of colour and tone in the distance, immediately create a sense of recession.*

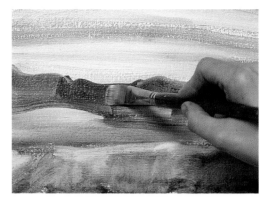

2 *Build up the shadows in the distant breaking wave and also in the foreground wave. The sand that the foreground wave has picked up makes the shadows in it much darker and browner.*

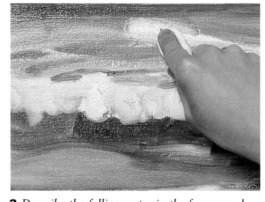

3 *Describe the falling water in the foreground wave with small, vertical strokes that counter the general horizontal arrangement of the waves. Make sure that the tonal extremes in the foreground wave are balanced, bringing up the highlights to match the deep shadows.*

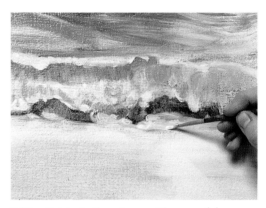

4 *The finished oil study provides a useful illustration of the effects of recession. You could continue to build up the surface in the same manner, making sure that you maintain the same level of progress across the whole painting.*

If you look out to sea, you can make out the details on those waves closest to you; the farther away the waves are, however, the less detail you can see, and waves in the far distance appear as a flat color. This is the effect of distance: the mind thinks that it sees individual waves in the distance because it knows they are there. If you paint them in, however, the eye will read them as being close to the picture plane, and give the water a vertical surface.

The "blueing" of the sea color and the reduction in tone over distance are also important for a feeling of recession. This effect is compounded by the natural configuration of the shore: where the water is shallow and the sun reflects off a sandy bottom, the water will look greener, whereas it will look bluer out to sea.

Waves also obey the laws of perspective in that the closer they are to the horizon, the closer together they will appear, so that in the distance they lose their individuality as they recede into the distance. The effects of recession will increase the lower the viewpoint you take; and seen from high above, the waves will be more evenly spaced for a greater distance.

Oil Pastels and Turpentine

Building a wave over an ultramarine-blue acrylic underpainting, the artist takes advantage both of the dry, almost waxy quality of these pastels, and of their painterly dimension blended with turpentine. This method of blending allows the colour to be moved around without flattening it in the later stages.

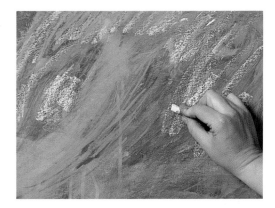

1 *Use broad pastel strokes, with the stick held on its side, over a dry acrylic underpainting, to describe the direction of the breaking wave and the distribution of tone.*

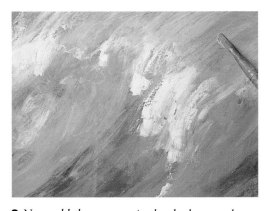

2 *Now add the greens – in the shadows under the curling crest and in the upper parts of the wave. They will be blended with white using turpentine at a later stage.*

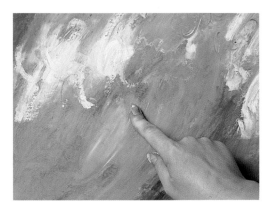

3 *Use a dark blue pastel to describe the eruption of power at the crest of the wave, working into the blended pastel, sgraffito-style, taking pastel away and applying pressure for a hint of blue.*

One of the most exciting experiences is to watch waves crashing onto rocks, to be thrown up in a jet of spray and spume. The expectation each time of a bigger explosion than the last, and the expression of the power of the water, cannot fail to thrill. Getting this across in a painting, however, requires some skill. The actual moment of impact and explosion is difficult to sketch, and though photographs are useful, the static nature of a wave caught at the moment of impact expresses better than any other subject the inadequacies of the medium. In a painting it is possible not only to record the moment of impact, but also to suggest what came before and what happened afterward, because the thrill of the moment and the expectations can be captured with expressive brushwork and textural techniques.

Watercolor embodies the translucency of the water with its myriad colors. Practice running colors and shades of colors into one another wet-in-wet to get a swirling, gradated wash for those indefinable colors at the base of a wave. You may find that marking out areas to reserve as white paper, to represent the foam, prevents you from expressing the movement of the water and the waves in the brushwork. If so, try reserving those areas with liquid frisket at the outset; or try adding the foam with opaque white gouache at the end; or take away the paint by scraping back to the white paper with a scalpel. Don't use the latter technique, however, for large areas.

Other techniques

With soft pastels, the immediacy of crashing waves can be conveyed if the colors are applied freshly, without too much blending or superimposition of one color on another. Try laying a watercolor wash first (on stretched watercolor paper), then break off pieces of pastel to use on their sides, making short strokes that interlock and sometimes overlap to indicate the fall of the light and the direction of the movement of the water. These strokes will contrast with the powerful explosion of spray from a crashing wave,

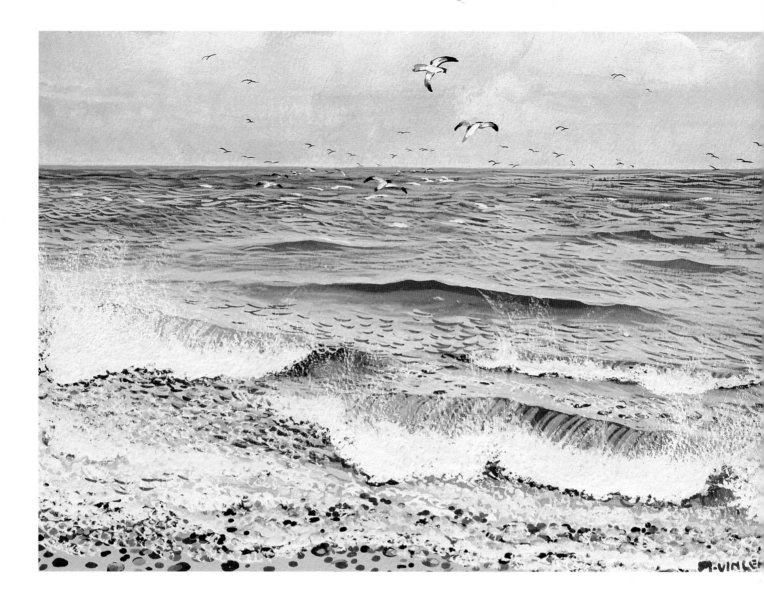

which can be created in expressive, directional strokes of tinted whites and grays. For textured spray, stipple with the end of the chalk, twisting as you take the stick away. Anything is permissible if it works: you could try to create the texture of the spume by filing chalk onto a layer of adhesive gum arabic. You could also work on the finest grade of sandpaper which will let you build up more layers of texture.

Oil pastels were made for rough seas. They can be mixed with turpentine for an expressive underpainting, which can be worked into with the dry sticks while it is still wet, and again when dry for a more chalky burst of spray.

The fast-drying quality of acrylic paints allows initial, thin washes and glazes to be laid down for the main color of the sea. These will dry quickly enough to let the white water be built up with heavy impasto, applied with a knife or any other instrument that comes to hand, all in one sitting.

The painter in oils will impress upon you that it is the fact that they don't dry too quickly that makes them so attractive, allowing time to move the paint around. Oil sketches done by building layers of thin paint wet-in-wet have a fluid quality that is very expressive of moving water.

▲ **Outgoing Tide, Kessingland**
(gouache)
MICHAEL VINCENT
Dry-brush textural techniques describe the foreground, contrasting with the flatter background. Note, too, the use of the gulls to lead the eye into the distance.

The color of the sea

We wonder at the aquamarine color of the sea in a coral cove yet we know that the color of water is affected by the surroundings and the quality of the light. The sea in a coral cove will combine the blue reflected from the sky and golden rays reflected off the yellow sandy seabed. In this section we look at how light, depth and surroundings affect the color of the sea.

Of course, to find such variations in the main color of the sea, you don't need to travel the world, as such chameleon-like behavior can occur in any harbor as a result of the slightest change in the weather. And you could find them all on the same day off the coast of Venezuela or in the Indian Ocean should the weather and the light decide to play tricks. No wonder the sea has us all in its thrall. But first, let us look at the conditions that affect the color of the sea.

Light and the sea

As in all paintings of water, the color of the prevailing light should affect your choice of color for the sea. You can choose to paint in a light that complements the mood of your painting – a cool, gray-blue light for a stormy sea, or a pinky morning light for a view across breakers on the Great Barrier Reef. This light will tint the white surf and can be continued throughout the painting. One way of doing this is to put a pink, yellow or gray wash over the paper, board or canvas so that color comes through in the sky, sea and shore as the light does. This underpainting can be allowed to show through subsequent layers of colors in places, or to qualify thin washes and glazes.

The prevailing light not only sets the pitch of the color, but also brings a painting

Dilute Acrylics
Acrylics can be used very dilute, almost like watercolour. Here, thin washes are superimposed one over another to create the subtle diversity of color in a view out to sea.

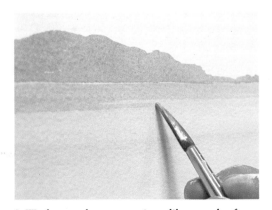

1 *Wash over the sea area in a dilute wash of ultramarine blue, making it paler towards the foreground. When the wash is dry, add another, stronger wash of the same blue, leaving an edge of pale blue where the sea abuts the land.*

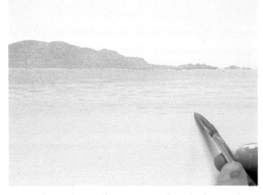

2 *Working down the painting, break the wash with small horizontal strokes for a change of colour and tone.*

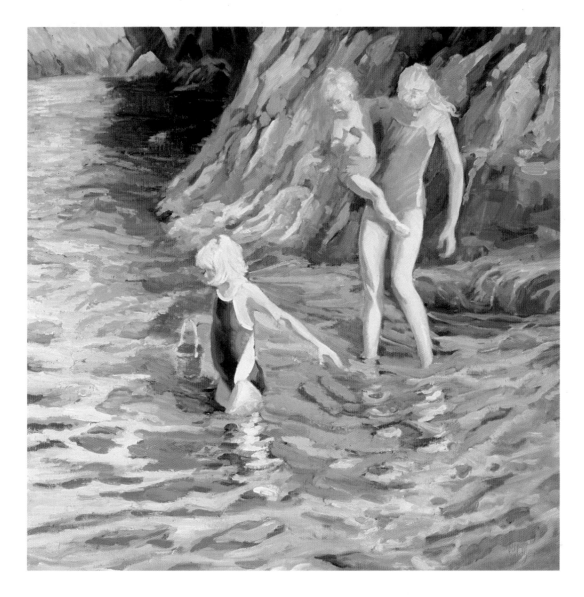

◄ **Sunshine Kids**

(oil)

DENISE BURNS

Reflections of the figures, rocks and sky are fragmented by the swell, giving little peepholes into the green-blue depths of the water below the surface. The subtleties of color and tone, built up in carefully placed strokes wet-in-wet, are well observed.

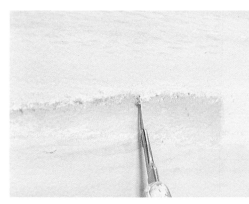

3 *Paint the wave in the foreground with a darker, greener blue tempered by the color of the sand. When this is dry, gently scrape back into the white paper with a sharp scalpel to produce the crest.*

4 *Take an opaque blue-white wash over the yellow sand where the water comes up over the sand. Note the horizontal touches of white, scraped back with the scalpel.*

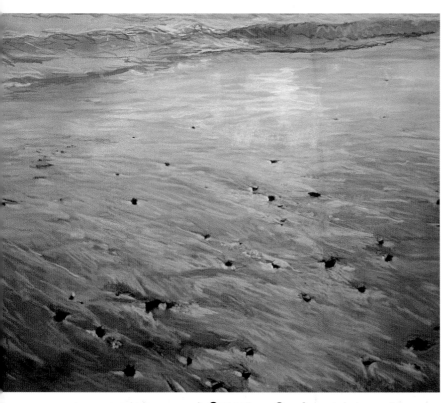

▲ **Sunset on Sand** (pastel on sandpaper)
KITTY WALLIS
The brilliant colours of the setting sun reflected in the wet sand eliminate the sentimentality associated with a full-blown sunset.

of the sea alive. Because of the many facets of a moving wave – tiny ripples, splashes of water, swirls and patches of white foam – points of reflected light of all shapes and sizes should be strewn across the painting. These patches of light are important to the composition, leading the eye from one part of the painting to another, and to the vitality of the painting.

Reflections and color

The color of the sea, like that of all water, is affected by its surroundings. Shallow water is qualified by the seabed – whether yellow sand or dark weed – whereas far out, the color is influenced by reflections of the sky. Even if it is not a mirror-like reflection, as produced by still water, facets of a moving wave will face and reflect the sky, and this becomes the overall "color" of the sea at that moment. The general color of the sea is usually darker than the sky, but disturbed, broken water that is full of air bubbles appears lighter. The sea is usually translucent, especially compared to a cloudy sky, so try not to add too much white, which will make the color too opaque.

Variations in the general overall color occur naturally and can be used by the artist

Prevailing Light Affecting Color

Try some experimental color mixing for seascapes, making swatches of graded tones created by the different lights you can find on these pages. Top: a golden light on the evening shore, in pastels. Middle: a cool, bright light in the mid-afternoon, in acrylics. Below: suffused pink light coming through the rain, in oils.

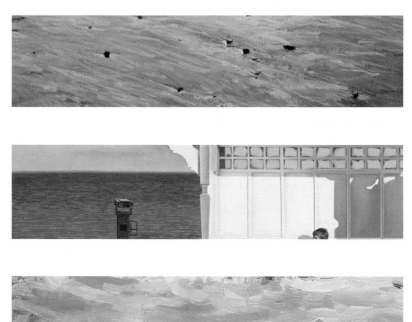

▶ **Clock Shelter**

(acrylic)

NICK HARRIS

*The background
view out to sea
offers an escape into
the distance from
the abrupt frontality
of the shelter. The
expanse of cool blue
sea is broken with
small horizontal
strokes of white,
with larger breaking
waves in the
foreground.*

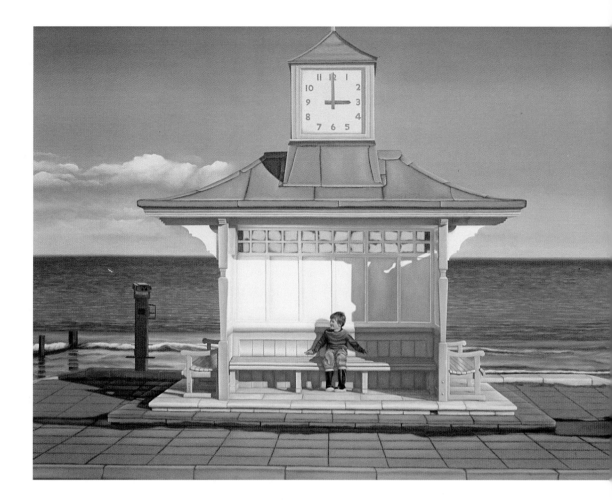

to break up an expanse of sea. On flatter
water, breezes can break up the surface of the
water in places, and the surface will appear
lighter as it reflects light from the sky. Rocks,
reefs and sandbanks can break the surface of
the water or cause the waves to break, and
this surf will make a lighter patch in the sea.
Cloud shadows, on the other hand, will
create a pattern of darker patches across the
surface, breaking the monotony.

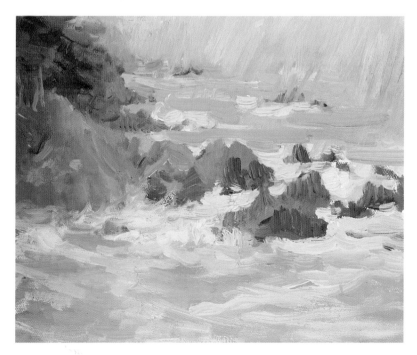

▲ **Rain, Rain, Go Away** (oil)

DENISE BURNS

*The suffused pink light breaking through the rain shower tints
the highlights on the breaking waves. This effect is explored in a
delicate range of colors and tone.*

PROJECT 5

Building up Layers of Paint

Working from a precise drawing, this dramatic view of the sea breaking over the pier is carefully built up with superimposed broken layers of paint, starting very dilute and getting thicker. Each layer sharpens up the image. You can see how the artist was conscious of the interplay between the strong horizontals in the composition (the cloud, top of the cliffs and the pier) and the verticals (the lighthouse and the cliffs) and how he chose a viewpoint which offset the lines of waves, introducing diagonals with the breakers and in the cloud.

Materials used

Acrylic fine grain paper 235, 20 × 16 inches

●

Acrylic paints: Payne's gray, cerulean, raw umber, cadmium red, viridian hue, phthalocyanine blue (Prussian)

●

Brushes: ½-inch flat, 1-inch long round

●

Pencil

●

Palette – piece of glass with a sheet of white paper beneath (easy to scrape off paint at the end)

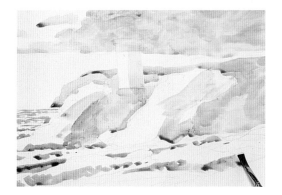

1 *The glaring white of the paper is killed off with thin washes of Payne's gray, cerulean and raw umber, roughly scrubbed in.*

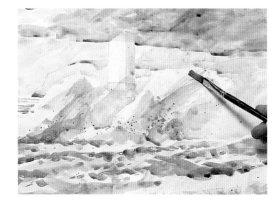

2 *The paper is covered except for the lighthouse and left to dry. Another thin layer adds some directional strokes in the breaking waves.*

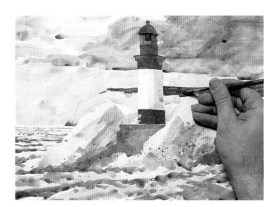

3 *The next layer is less dilute and the artist cuts out the shapes with horizontal strokes of the square-ended brush. Dark shadows are cut in around the waves.*

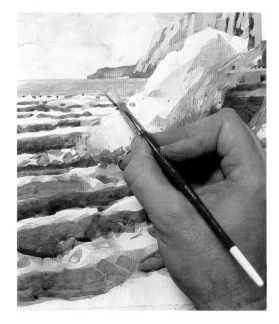

4 *The sky is built up with a thin layer, scrubbed on unevenly, paler toward the horizon and the blue taken down to the sea where it is painted over the distant waves. Touches of blue, reflections of the sky, are then taken forward, more concentrated in the foreground.*

5 White is cut into the shadow for the highlights, qualified in places by the underpainting. The brush is rolled into the waves for touches of impasto.

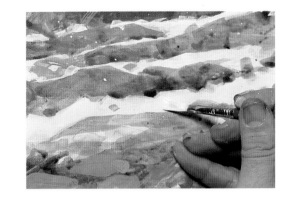

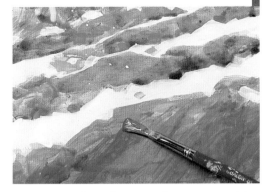

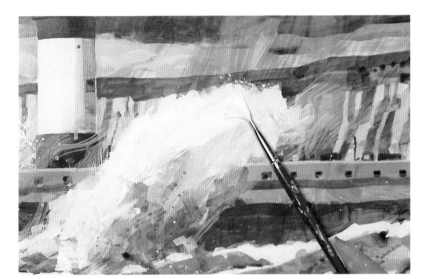

6 To reinforce the sense of recession, making the foreground darker, crisper and more intense, the color of the nearest wave is built up with a scrubbing motion. This depth of color comes from successive layers of broken color.

7 Scumbled strokes of dry white for the spray are taken over the shadows, the pier and the cliffs with a few flicks of the brush. Then thicker white is rolled on for impasto highlights. These ridges of paint catch the light adding to the subtlety of this white water.

▶ **Freak Waves**

IAN SIDAWAY

The heavy cloud comes to dominate the painting with a powerful sense of foreboding. It is built up with final thin washes making it more three-dimensional. The hard horizontal line of the cloud's base is softened with shafts of falling rain, connecting it to the landscape. A sense of recession is created by the waves on the left getting closer together and less distinct in the distance.

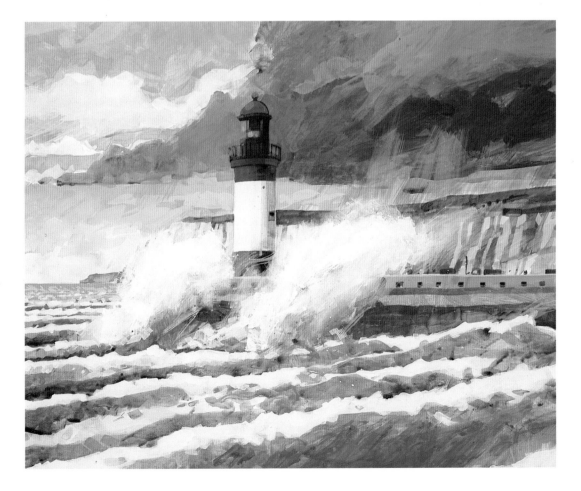

Building up Washes

The ultimate palm-fringed tropical shore with a view out to sea is built up in watercolors with delicate washes wet-in-wet and wet-on-dry. Having reserved some of the white areas of surf with liquid frisket, the bones of the composition are mapped out in thin washes of color, never letting the color dry flat (and remembering it dries paler). The breaking waves in the foreground are then built up in superimposed patches wet-on-dry. The tricky area of the water lapping the sand develops from small touches of color superimposed wet-on-dry.

Materials used

Watercolor paints: viridian green, ultramarine blue, cobalt blue, raw sienna, light red, cadmium yellow

●

Light pencil

●

Liquid frisket

●

Brushes: No 6 and No 2 sable, watercolor brushes

●

Eraser

●

Ceramic mixing dish

●

Two water containers – one for diluting paints and one for cleaning brushes

●

Paper towels

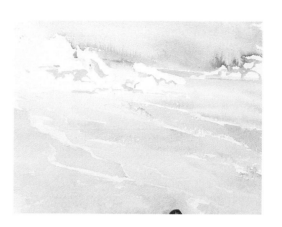

1 Sketch in the composition with a pencil and apply liquid frisket for the highlights. Apply pale washes to the sky, sea and sand, painting the water wet-in-wet with ultramarine and viridian.

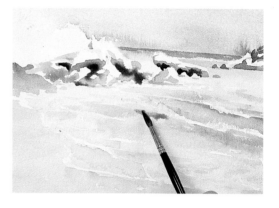

2 The foreground colors are strengthened with stronger washes wet-on-dry. Deeper and darker blue sea on the horizon is applied wet-on-dry with washes of viridian.

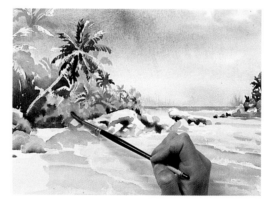

3 The vegetation is built up in three tones of green. Darker shadows (viridian and ultramarine blue) are soft edged as the preceding layer of dried paint is wetted before feeding in the color.

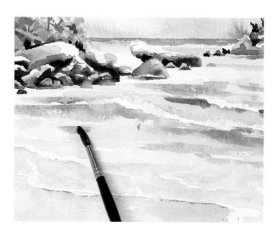

4 The liquid frisket is removed with a clean eraser and touches of blue are added to the foreground waves. Where the water spreads over the sand, patches of drybrush are added in viridian and raw sienna.

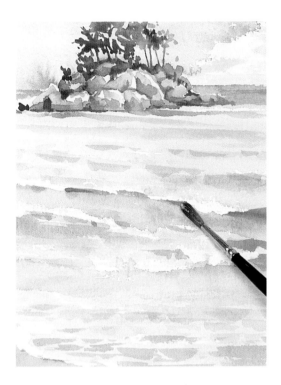

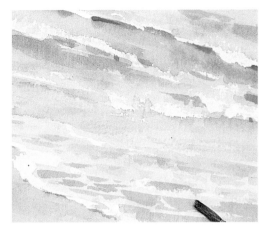

5 Now the waves are coming together but to balance the brightness of the surf, the shadows need to be darker but don't hurry this development. Starker shadows with hard edges are added wet-on-dry, but for softer edges wet the surface first with water or blot with a tissue.

6 Returning to the water's edge, further darker patches of neutral green are added. The gradual build-up of superimposed patches of increasingly concentrated paint captures the thin, translucent wash of foam-streaked water.

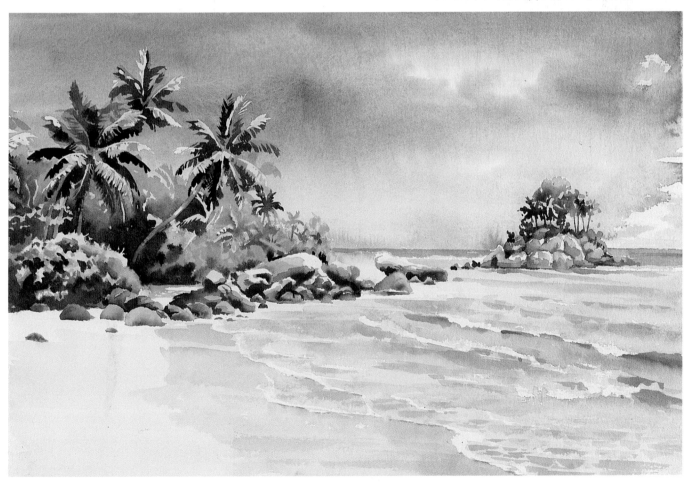

▲ **Tropical Cove**

HAZEL SOAN

The artist has built up the foreground waves, working on their three-dimensionality and the translucency of the water.

PROJECT

7

Fair Boating Weather

The design is taken from the imagination with the horizon crooked to emphasize the rocking of the boat, further projected by the strong diagonals in the composition. The stretch of sea to the horizon contrasts with the busy composition of the boat but it is carefully divided into three areas of foreground, middle ground, and background, each treated differently. This area of sea is built up intuitively, balancing tones in an abstract pattern. A pale yellow evening light suffuses the picture unifying the various parts.

Materials used

Chalk pastels: various colors and tints, and various sizes of chalk, the larger ones in this case are softer and smoother, the smaller ones, drier and sharper. The artist picks out a selection in his left hand from a vast array for a particular area, returning them to the tray for another selection.

●

Pastel canvas dry-mounted onto board

●

Pencil

●

Eraser

●

Hand mirror

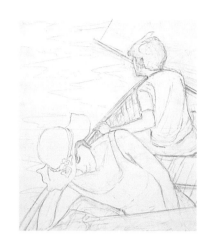

1 *With a pencil, draw up the composition. As it comes from the imagination, the structure may need fine tuning as you go along, adjusting lines to make the composition work.*

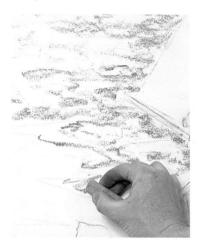

2 *Start with the sea, feeling for the colors and tones in loose strokes.*

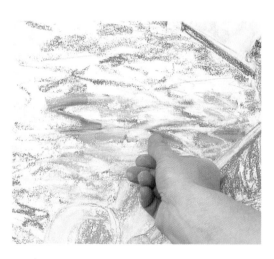

3 *Continue to block in the whole picture with loose color to get a feeling for it and then return to the sea to start building it up. Work in a second tone of blue, blending it with your thumb.*

4 *Now add darker and lighter blues blended with off-whites and letting the canvas show through as highlights. For larger areas, such as the sail, use the side of the hand to blend the strokes.*

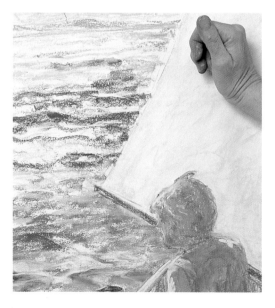

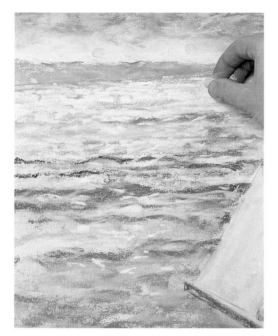

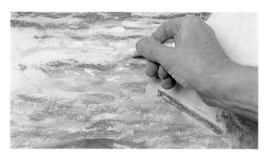

6 *Add palest lemon yellow highlights, using an edge of the chalk and pulling away cleanly to get a bright mark.*

5 The strokes for the waves in the distance are made with small, jabbing strokes. Add touches of pale lemon yellow to the sea which is well divided through tone and color into foreground, middle ground and background.

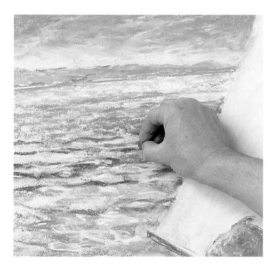

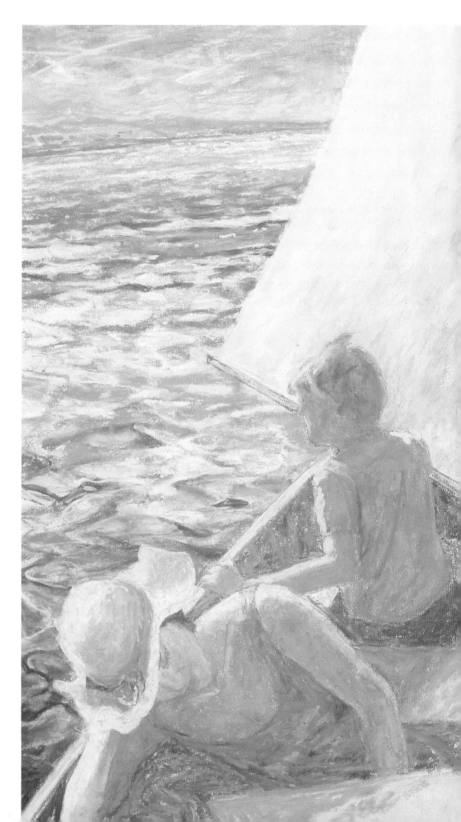

7 At this stage it is a good idea to get an objective view of your work by looking at it in a hand mirror. The middle ground section of the sea has been "lost," so redefine it with darker contrasts and a touch of blue-green.

▶ **Evening Sail**

PATRICK CULLEN

The figures and the boat pick up colors from the picture – lemon yellow, ultramarine blue, aquamarine and the neutral tones of the far strip of land.

Index

Credits

Quarto Publishing would like to thank all the artists who have kindly allowed us to reproduce their work in this book.

Location photographs included appear by courtesy of Julian Bray, Jo Carlill, Nick Clark, Moira Clinch, John Hallowes, Giulia Hetherington, Susannah Jayes and Patricia Seligman. All other photographs are the copyright of Quarto Publishing.

Finally, we would also like to acknowledge and thank the following artists for their help in the demonstrations of techniques: Patrick Cullen, William Garfit, Margaret Glass, Paul Kenny, Debra Manifold, Kay Ohsten, Karen Rainey, Lincoln Seligman, Ian Sidaway, and Hazel Soan.